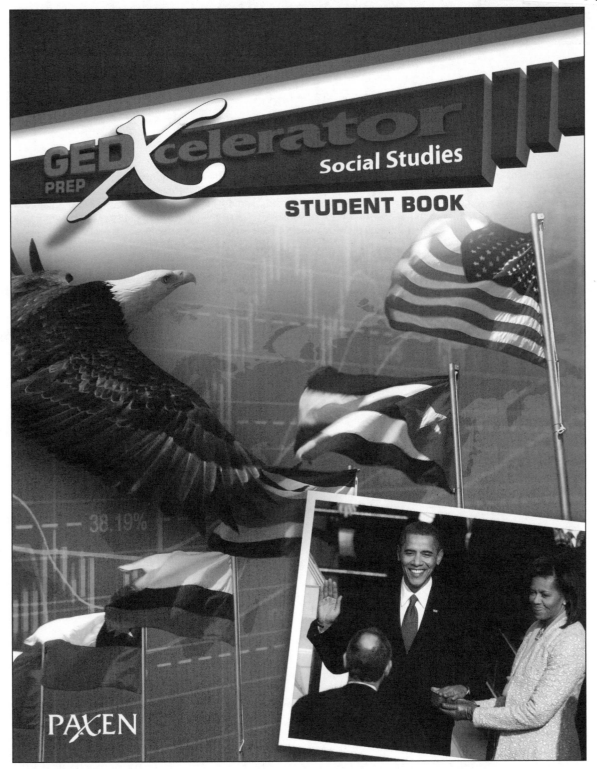

GED **X**celerator
PREP

Social Studies

STUDENT BOOK

PAXEN

PAXEN

Melbourne, Florida
www.paxen.com

Acknowledgements

For each of the selections and images listed below, grateful acknowledgement is made for permission to excerpt and/or reprint original or copyrighted material, as follows:

Text

75 Used with the permission of Columbia Encyclopedia. **84** Museum of the Moving Image, The Living Room Candidate (livingroomcandidate.org). **85** From *Chicago Tribune,* October 17, 2004 © Chicago Tribune. All rights reserved. Used by permission and protected by the Copyright Laws of the United States. The printing, copying, redistribution, or retransmission of the Material without express written permission is prohibited. **91** From *The New York Times,* September 18, 2008 © The New York Times. All rights reserved. Used by permission and protected by the Copyright Laws of the United States. The printing, copying, redistribution, or retransmission of the Material without express written permission is prohibited.

Images

(cover, flags) iStockphoto. **(cover, Obama)** Jim Young/Reuters/Corbis. **(cover, eagle)** Shutterstock Images. **(cover, world map)** iStockphoto. **(cover, financial diagrams)** iStockphoto. **v** iStockphoto. **vi** iStockphoto. **x** Jamie Carroll/iStockphoto. **BLIND** Metropolitan Transportation Commission. **20** Peter Turnley/Corbis. **45** Used with the permission of the Herb Block Foundation. **48** Yutaka Nagata/UN Photos. **68** Chip Somodevilla/Getty Images. **81** Used with the permission of David J. Frent/Political Americana. **83** Copyright by Bill Mauldin (1958). Courtesy of the Bill Mauldin Estate LLC. **91** Used with the permission of the Herb Block Foundation. **92** Copyright by Bill Mauldin (1962). Courtesy of the Bill Mauldin Estate LLC. **96** Used with the permission of CartoonStock.com. **112** Bettmann/Corbis.

ISBN-13: 978-1-934350-26-3
ISBN-10: 1-934350-26-5

2 3 4 5 6 7 8 9 10 GEDXSE3 16 15 14 13 12 11 10   Printed in the U.S.A.

GED PREP XCELERATOR

Social Studies Student Book

Table of Contents

About the GED Tests

Simply by turning to this page, you've made a decision that will change your life for the better. Each year, thousands of people just like you decide to pursue the General Education Development (GED) certificate. Like you, they left school for one reason or another. And now, just like them, you've decided to continue your education by studying for and taking the GED Tests.

However, the GED Tests are no easy task. The tests—five in all, spread across the subject areas of Language Arts/Reading, Language Arts/Writing, Mathematics, Science, and Social Studies—cover slightly more than seven hours. Preparation time takes considerably longer. The payoff, however, is significant: more and better career options, higher earnings, and the sense of achievement that comes with a GED certificate. Employers and colleges and universities accept the GED certificate as they would a high school diploma. On average, GED recipients earn more than $4,000 per year than do employees without a GED certificate.

The GED Tests have been constructed by the American Council on Education (ACE) to mirror a high-school curriculum. Although you will not need to know all of the information typically taught in high school, you will need to answer a variety of questions in specific subject areas. In Language Arts/Writing, you will need to write an essay on a topic of general knowledge.

In all cases, you will need to effectively read and follow directions, correctly interpret questions, and critically examine answer options. The table below details the five subject areas, the amount of questions within each of them, and the time that you will have to answer them. Since different states have different requirements for the amount of tests you may take in a single day, you will need to check with your local adult education center for requirements in your state or territory.

The original GED Tests were released in 1942 and since have been revised a total of three times. In each case, revisions to the tests have occurred as a result of educational findings or workplace needs. All told, more than 17 million people have received a GED certificate since the tests' inception.

SUBJECT AREA BREAKDOWN	CONTENT AREAS	ITEMS	TIME LIMIT
Language Arts/Reading	Literary texts—75% Nonfiction texts—25%	40 questions	65 minutes
Language Arts/Writing (Editing)	Organization—15% Sentence Structure—30% Usage—30% Mechanics—25%	50 questions	75 minutes
Language Arts/Writing (Essay)	Essay	Essay	45 minutes
Mathematics	Number Sense/Operations—20% to 30% Data Measurement/Analysis—20% to 30% Algebra—20% to 30% Geometry—20% to 30%	Part I: 25 questions (with calculator) Part II: 25 questions (without calculator)	90 minutes
Science	Life Science—45% Earth/Space Science—20% Physical Science—35%	50 questions	80 minutes
Social Studies	Geography—15% U.S. History—25% World History—15% U.S. Government/Civics—25% Economics—20%	50 questions	70 minutes

Three of the subject-area tests—Language Arts/Reading, Science, and Social Studies—will require you to answer questions by interpreting passages. The Science and Social Studies Tests also require you to interpret tables, charts, graphs, diagrams, timelines, political cartoons, and other visuals. In Language Arts/Reading, you also will need to answer questions based on workplace and consumer texts. The Mathematics Test, will require you to use basic computation, analysis, and reasoning skills to solve a variety of word problems, many of them involving graphics. On all of the tests, questions will be multiple-choice with five answer options. An example follows.

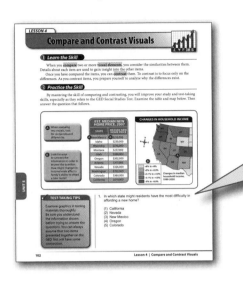

1. In which state might residents have the most difficulty in affording a new home?

(1) California
(2) Nevada
(3) New Mexico
(4) Oregon
(5) Colorado

On the Mathematics Test, you will have additional ways in which to register your responses to multiple-choice questions.

As the table on p. iv indicates, the Language Arts/Writing Test contains two parts, one for editing, the other for essay. In the editing portion of Language Arts/Writing, you will be asked to identify and correct common errors in various passages and texts while also deciding on the most effective organization of a text. In the essay portion, you will write an essay that provides an explanation or an opinion on a single topic of general knowledge.

Now that you understand the task at hand—and the benefits of a GED certificate—you must prepare for the GED Tests. In the pages that follow, you will find a recipe of sorts that, if followed, will help guide you toward successful completion of your GED certificate. So turn the page. The next chapter of your life begins right now.

About *GED Prep Xcelerator*

Along with choosing to pursue your GED certificate, you've made another smart decision by selecting *GED Prep Xcelerator* as your main study and preparation tool. Simply by purchasing *GED Prep Xcelerator*, you've joined an elite club with thousands of members, all with a common goal—earning their GED certificates. In this case, membership most definitely has its privileges.

For more than 65 years, the GED Tests have offered a second chance to people who need it most. To date, 17 million Americans like you have studied for and earned GED certificates and, in so doing, jump-started their lives and careers. Benefits abound for GED holders: Recent studies have shown that people with GED certificates earn more money, enjoy better health, and exhibit greater interest in and understanding of the world around them than those without.

In addition, more than 60 percent of GED recipients plan to further their educations, which will provide them with more and better career options. As if to underscore the point, U.S. Department of Labor projections show that 90 percent of the fastest-growing jobs through 2014 will require postsecondary education.

Your pathway to the future—a brighter future—begins now, on this page, with *GED Prep Xcelerator*, an intense, accelerated approach to GED preparation. Unlike other programs, which take months to teach the GED Tests through a content-based approach, *Xcelerator* gets to the heart of the GED Tests—and quickly—by emphasizing *concepts*. That's because at their core, the majority of the GED Tests are reading-comprehension exams. You must be able to read and interpret excerpts, passages, and various visuals—tables, charts, graphs, timelines, and so on—and then answer questions based upon them.

Xcelerator shows you the way. By emphasizing key reading and thinking concepts, *Xcelerator* equips learners like you with the skills and strategies you'll need to correctly interpret and answer questions on the GED Tests. Two-page micro-lessons in each student book provide focused and efficient instruction, while call-out boxes, sample exercises, and test-taking and other thinking strategies aid in understanding complex concepts. For those who require additional support, we offer the *Xcelerator* workbooks, which provide twice the support and practice exercises as the student books.

Unlike other GED materials, which were designed for the classroom, *Xcelerator* materials were designed *from* the classroom, using proven educational theory and cutting-edge classroom philosophy. The result: More than 90 percent of people who study with *Xcelerator* earn their GED certificates. For learners who have long had the deck stacked against them, the odds are finally in their favor. And yours.

GED BY THE NUMBERS

17 million
Number of GED recipients since the inception of GED Tests

1.23 million
Amount of students who fail to graduate from high school each year

700,000
Number of GED test-takers each year

451,759
Total number of students who passed the GED Tests in 2007

$4,000
Average additional earnings per year for GED recipients

About *GED Prep Xcelerator Social Studies*

Some people who have taken the GED Social Studies Test have been surprised by how difficult it was. While the test assesses your ability to understand and interpret subject-specific text or graphics, you also need some basic geographical and historical knowledge. On pages x–xiii, you will learn to use logic and reasoning to help you assess information and graphics on the Social Studies Test. You will have a total of 70 minutes to answer 50 multiple-choice questions organized across five main content areas: Geography (15% of all questions), U.S. History (25%), World History (15%), U.S. Government/Civics (25%), and Economics (20%). Material in *GED Prep Xcelerator Social Studies* has been organized with these percentages in mind.

GED Prep Xcelerator Social Studies helps deconstruct the different elements of the test by helping people like you build and develop key reading and thinking skills. A combination of targeted strategies, informational call-outs and sample questions, key geographic terms, assorted tips and hints (including Test-Taking Tips, Using Logic, and Making Assumptions), and many test-like questions help to clearly focus your efforts in needed areas, all with an eye toward the end goal: Success on the GED Tests. As on the GED Science Test, the GED Social Studies Test uses the thinking skills of *comprehension, analysis, application,* and *evaluation.*

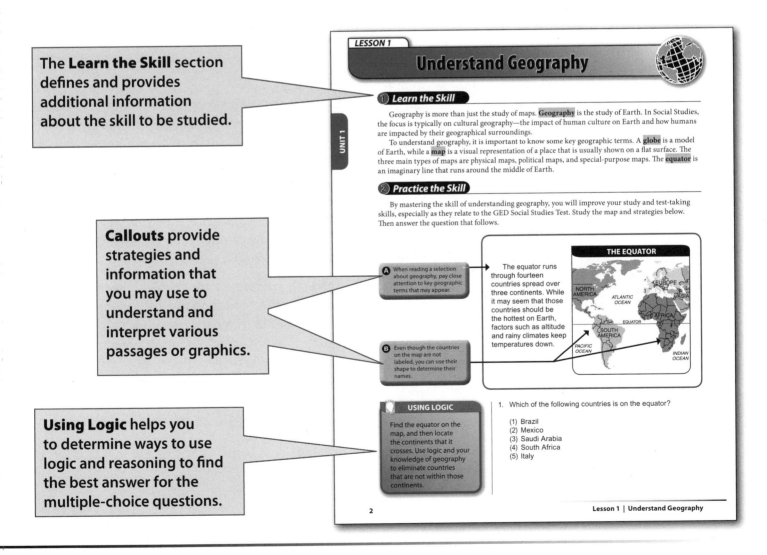

The **Learn the Skill** section defines and provides additional information about the skill to be studied.

Callouts provide strategies and information that you may use to understand and interpret various passages or graphics.

Using Logic helps you to determine ways to use logic and reasoning to find the best answer for the multiple-choice questions.

LESSON 1

Understand Geography

① Learn the Skill

Geography is more than just the study of maps. **Geography** is the study of Earth. In Social Studies, the focus is typically on cultural geography—the impact of human culture on Earth and how humans are impacted by their geographical surroundings.

To understand geography, it is important to know some key geographic terms. A **globe** is a model of Earth, while a **map** is a visual representation of a place that is usually shown on a flat surface. The three main types of maps are physical maps, political maps, and special-purpose maps. The **equator** is an imaginary line that runs around the middle of Earth.

② Practice the Skill

By mastering the skill of understanding geography, you will improve your study and test-taking skills, especially as they relate to the GED Social Studies Test. Study the map and strategies below. Then answer the question that follows.

A When reading a selection about geography, pay close attention to key geographic terms that may appear.

The equator runs through fourteen countries spread over three continents. While it may seem that those countries should be the hottest on Earth, factors such as altitude and rainy climates keep temperatures down.

THE EQUATOR

B Even though the countries on the map are not labeled, you can use their shape to determine their names.

USING LOGIC

Find the equator on the map, and then locate the continents that it crosses. Use logic and your knowledge of geography to eliminate countries that are not within those continents.

1. Which of the following countries is on the equator?

(1) Brazil
(2) Mexico
(3) Saudi Arabia
(4) South Africa
(5) Italy

Lesson 1 | Understand Geography

2

Test-Taking Tips

The GED Tests include 240 questions across the five subject-area exams of Language Arts/Reading, Language Arts/Writing, Mathematics, Science, and Social Studies. In each of the GED Tests, you will need to apply some amount of subject-area knowledge. However, because all of the questions are multiple-choice items largely based on text or visuals (such as tables, charts, or graphs), the emphasis in *GED Prep Xcelerator* is on helping learners like you build and develop core reading and thinking skills. As part of the overall strategy, various test-taking tips are included below and throughout the book to help you improve your performance on the GED Tests. For example:

◆ *Always thoroughly read the directions so that you know exactly what to do.* In Mathematics, for example, one part of the test allows for the use of a calculator. The other part does not. If you are unsure of what to do, ask the test provider if the directions can be explained.

◆ *Read each question carefully so that you fully understand what it is asking.* Some questions, for example, may present more information than you need to correctly answer them. Other questions may note emphasis through capitalized and boldfaced words (Which of the following is **NOT** an example of photosynthesis?).

◆ *Manage your time with each question.* Because the GED Tests are timed exams, you'll want to spend enough time with each question, but not *too* much time. For example, on the GED Science Test, you will have 80 minutes in which to answer 50 multiple-choice questions. That works out to a little more than 90 seconds per item. You can save time by first reading each question and its answer options before reading the passage or examining the graphic. Once you understand what the question is asking, review the passage or visual for the appropriate information.

◆ *Note any unfamiliar words in questions.* First attempt to re-read a question by omitting any unfamiliar word(s). Next, try to substitute another word in its place.

◆ *Answer all questions, regardless of whether you know the answer or are guessing at it.* There is no benefit in leaving questions unanswered on the GED Tests. Keep in mind the time that you have for each test and manage it accordingly. For time purposes, you may decide to initially skip questions. However, note them with a light mark beside the question and try to return to them before the end of the test.

◆ *Narrow answer options by re-reading each question and the accompanying text or graphic.* Although all five answers are possible, keep in mind that only one of them is correct. You may be able to eliminate one or two answers immediately; others may take more time and involve the use of either logic or assumptions. In some cases, you may need to make your best guess between two options. If so, keep in mind that test-makers often avoid answer patterns; that is, if you know the previous answer is (2) and are unsure of the answer to the next question but have narrowed it to options (2) and (4), you may want to choose (4).

◆ *Read all answer choices.* Even though the first or second answer choice may appear to be correct, be sure to thoroughly read all five answer choices. Then go with your instinct when answering questions. For example, if your first instinct is to mark (1) in response to a question, it's best to stick with that answer unless you later determine that answer to be incorrect. Usually, the first answer you choose is the correct one.

◆ *Correctly complete your answer sheet by marking one numbered space on the answer sheet beside the number to which it corresponds.* Mark only one answer for each item; multiple answers will be scored as incorrect. If time permits, double-check your answer sheet after completing the test to ensure that you have made as many marks— no more, no less—as there are questions.

Study Skills

You've already made two very smart decisions in trying to earn your GED certificate and in purchasing *GED Prep Xcelerator* to help you do so. The following are additional strategies to help you optimize success on the GED Tests.

3 weeks out . . .

- Set a study schedule for the GED Tests. Choose times in which you are most alert, and places, such as a library, that provide the best study environment.

- Thoroughly review all material in *GED Prep Xcelerator*, using the *GED Prep Xcelerator Social Studies Workbook* to extend understanding of concepts in the *GED Prep Xcelerator Social Studies Student Book*.

- Make sure you have the necessary tools for the job: sharpened pencils, pens, paper, and, for Mathematics, the Casio-FX 260 Solar calculator.

- Keep notebooks for each of the subject areas you are studying. Folders with pockets are useful for storing loose papers.

- When taking notes, restate thoughts or ideas in your own words rather than copying them directly from a book. You can phrase these notes as complete sentences, as questions (with answers), or as fragments, provided you understand them.

- Take the pretests, noting any troublesome subject areas. Focus your remaining study around those subject areas.

1 week out . . .

- Prepare the items you will need for the GED Tests: admission ticket (if necessary), acceptable form of identification, some sharpened No. 2 pencils (with erasers), a watch, eyeglasses (if necessary), a sweater or jacket, and a high-protein snack to eat during breaks.

- Map out the course to the test center, and visit it a day or two before your scheduled exam. If you drive, find a place to park at the center.

- Get a good night's sleep the night before the GED Tests. Studies have shown that learners with sufficient rest perform better in testing situations.

The day of . . .

- Eat a hearty breakfast high in protein. As with the rest of your body, your brain needs ample energy to perform well.

- Arrive 30 minutes early to the testing center. This will allow sufficient time in the event of a change to a different testing classroom.

- Pack a sizeable lunch, especially if you plan to be at the testing center most of the day.

- Focus and relax. You've come this far, spending weeks preparing and studying for the GED Tests. It's your time to shine.

Before You Begin: Using Logic and Making Assumptions

At more than seven hours in length, the GED Tests are to testing what marathons are to running. Just like marathons, though, you may train for success on the GED Tests. As you know, the exams test your ability to interpret and answer questions about various passages and visual elements. Your ability to answer such questions involves the development and use of core reading and thinking skills. Chief among these are the skills of reasoning, logic, and assumptions.

Reasoning involves the ability to explain and describe ideas. **Logic** is the science of correct reasoning. Together, reasoning and logic guide our ability to make and understand assumptions. An **assumption** is a belief that we know to be true and which we use to understand the world around us.

You use logic and make assumptions every day, sometimes without even knowing that you're doing so. For example, you might go to bed one night knowing that your car outside is dry; you might awaken the next morning to discover that your car is wet. In that example, it would be *reasonable* for you to *assume* that your car is wet because it rained overnight. Even though you did not see it rain, it is the most *logical* explanation for the change in the car's appearance.

When thinking logically about items on the GED Tests, you identify the consequences, or answers, from text or visuals. Next, you determine whether the text or visuals logically and correctly support the consequences. If so, they are considered valid. If not, they are considered invalid. For example, read the following text and determine whether each passage is valid or invalid.

Passage A

The GED Tests assess a person's reading comprehension skills. Ellen enjoys reading. Therefore, Ellen will do well on the GED Tests.

Passage B

The GED Tests cover material in five different subject areas. Aaron has geared his studies toward the tests, and he has done well on practice tests. Therefore, Aaron may do well on the GED Tests.

Each of the above situations has a consequence: *Ellen will* or *Aaron may do well* on the GED Tests. By using reasoning and logic, you can make an assumption about which consequence is valid. In the example above, it is unreasonable to assume that Ellen will do well on the GED Tests simply because she likes to read. However, it is reasonable to assume that Aaron may do well on the GED Tests because he studied for and did well on the practice tests in each of the five subject areas.

Use the same basic principles of reasoning, logic, and assumption to determine which answer option logically and correctly supports the question on the GED Social Studies Test. You may find occasions in which you have narrowed the field of possible correct answers to two, from which you must make a best, educated guess. In such cases, weigh both options and determine the one that, reasonably, makes the most sense.

You can apply these same skills when analyzing the questions on the GED Social Studies Test. Use the sample question, annotated responses, and callouts below to begin developing your logic and reasoning skills. On the pages that follow, use these same strategies to analyze the questions. Remember to think about the most *reasonable* and *logical* conclusions or consequences before making any *assumptions*.

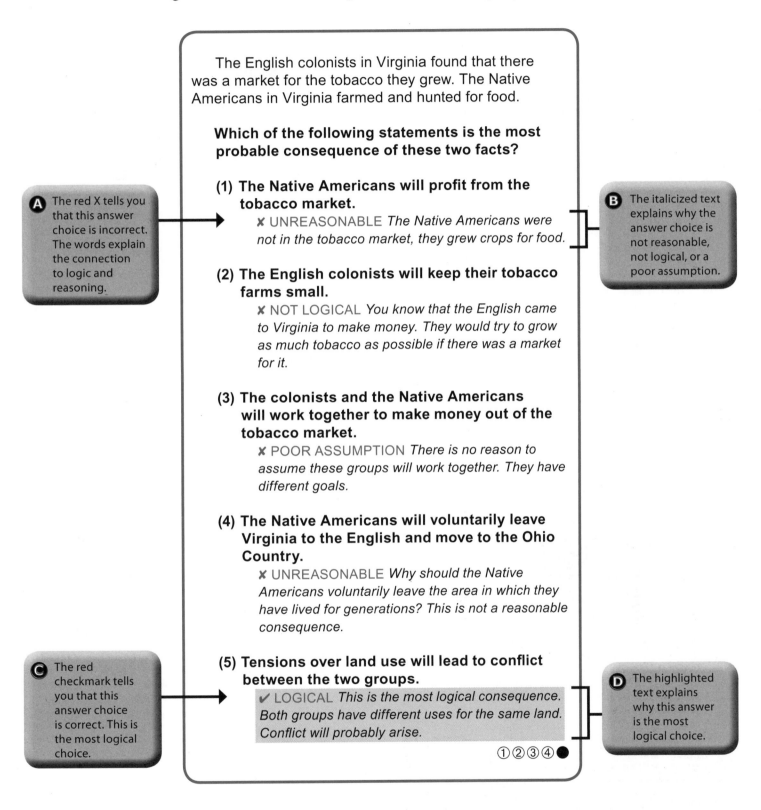

The English colonists in Virginia found that there was a market for the tobacco they grew. The Native Americans in Virginia farmed and hunted for food.

Which of the following statements is the most probable consequence of these two facts?

(1) The Native Americans will profit from the tobacco market.

✗ UNREASONABLE *The Native Americans were not in the tobacco market, they grew crops for food.*

(2) The English colonists will keep their tobacco farms small.

✗ NOT LOGICAL *You know that the English came to Virginia to make money. They would try to grow as much tobacco as possible if there was a market for it.*

(3) The colonists and the Native Americans will work together to make money out of the tobacco market.

✗ POOR ASSUMPTION *There is no reason to assume these groups will work together. They have different goals.*

(4) The Native Americans will voluntarily leave Virginia to the English and move to the Ohio Country.

✗ UNREASONABLE *Why should the Native Americans voluntarily leave the area in which they have lived for generations? This is not a reasonable consequence.*

(5) Tensions over land use will lead to conflict between the two groups.

✔ LOGICAL *This is the most logical consequence. Both groups have different uses for the same land. Conflict will probably arise.*

① ② ③ ④ ●

A The red X tells you that this answer choice is incorrect. The words explain the connection to logic and reasoning.

B The italicized text explains why the answer choice is not reasonable, not logical, or a poor assumption.

C The red checkmark tells you that this answer choice is correct. This is the most logical choice.

D The highlighted text explains why this answer is the most logical choice.

These additional sample questions will assess your understanding of logic, reasoning, and assumptions. If you need help, annotated answers are located at the bottom of the page. You will have many more opportunities to answer questions using logic, reasoning, and assumptions throughout the *GED Prep Xcelerator Social Studies Student Book.*

Directions: Choose the <u>one best answer</u> to each question.

Question 1 refers to the following information.

In the 1790s, many Americans settled in the areas immediately west of the Appalachian Mountains.
[HINT: The date provides a clue. Locations are also helpful. Remember that the Appalachian Mountains run from western New York and Pennsylvania down into South Carolina.]

1. What event caused this growth in settlement?

    (1) the French and Indian War
    (2) the Proclamation of 1763
    (3) the American Revolution
    (4) the Louisiana Purchase
    (5) the Civil War

    ① ② ③ ④ ⑤

Question 2 refers to the following map.

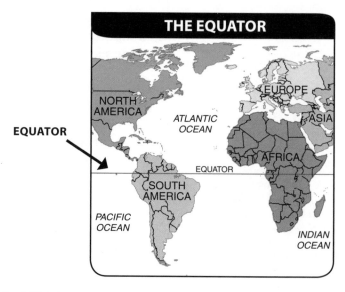

2. Which country is on the equator?
    [HINT: This question asks about a country, not a continent. The countries on the map are not labeled. You will have to use logic to find the answer]

    (1) the United States
    (2) Spain
    (3) China
    (4) Kenya
    (5) Cuba

    ① ② ③ ④ ⑤

Answers

1. (1) ✘ POOR ASSUMPTION While the colonists may have thought they could settle in the area after the French and Indian War, the British forbade them. This was one of the reasons the colonists wanted independence.
    (2) ✘ UNREASONABLE Do not be drawn in by an answer with a date. Remember that the proclamation forbid colonists from settling west of the Appalachian Mountains. Also, it was seventeen years before the settlement.
    (3) ✔ LOGICAL The American Revolution ended in 1783. The Americans gained the territory west of the Appalachians from the British and opened the area to settlement. This event was the closest to the 1790s.
    (4) ✘ NOT LOGICAL The Louisiana Purchase included land west of the Mississippi River, not the Appalachian Mountains. The purchase was not made until 1803.
    (5) ✘ UNREASONABLE The Civil War occurred in the 1800s.

2. (1) ✘ UNREASONABLE The United States is in North America. The equator does not cross North America.
    (2) ✘ UNREASONABLE Spain is in Europe. The equator does not cross Europe.
    (3) ✘ NOT LOGICAL China is in Asia. While the equator does cross parts of Asia, China is probably too far north. Also, China is not shown on this map.
    (4) ✔ LOGICAL Kenya is in Africa. The equator crosses several African countries. Kenya is the only African country that is a choice. It is the most logical answer.
    (5) ✘ UNREASONABLE Cuba is an island off the coast of Florida. Looking at the map, the islands near Florida are not on the equator.

Question 3 refers to the following information.

Britain and France lost over 2.5 million men during World War I.

3. How might this explain their relationship with Hitler's Germany in the 1930s?
   [HINT: Think about how Britain and France first reacted when Hitler used aggressive tactics to take over other European countries before World War II.]

The British and the French

(1) declared war immediately when Hitler was elected chancellor of Germany
(2) did not want to have another costly war, so they appeased Hitler
(3) believed that their dead from World War I would have died in vain if Hitler was allowed to invade Poland
(4) felt guilty that they were not more punitive towards Germany after World War I
(5) began a massive military build-up and eagerly waited for another war

①②③④⑤

Question 4 refers to the following information.

U.S. Constitution Amendment I

Congress shall make no law respecting an establishment of religion, or prohibiting the free exercise thereof; or abridging the freedom of speech, or of the press; or the right of the people peaceably to assemble, and to petition the government for a redress of grievances.

4. Which of the following would be a violation of the First Amendment?
   [HINT: This question is asking for a "violation" of the amendment, so look for an act that the amendment forbids.]

(1) Congress declares Protestantism the official religion of the United States
(2) college student protestors hold a peaceful rally
(3) Catholics hold mass in St. Patrick Church in Washington, D.C.
(4) a newspaper reporter writes a negative article about the president
(5) a convicted felon sends a petition to the Supreme Court

①②③④⑤

Answers

3. (1) ✗ UNREASONABLE Hitler was elected chancellor in 1932. World War II began in 1939.
   (2) ✔ LOGICAL/BEST ASSUMPTION Both France and Britain were still recovering from the effects of World War I. They were anxious to do whatever it took to prevent another war, so they allowed Hitler to take over some countries.
   (3) ✗ POOR ASSUMPTION Yes, the British and the French lost a lot of men in World War I, but did everything they could to avoid another war.
   (4) ✗ NOT LOGICAL Hitler's rise to power can be connected with the allies' punitive treatment of Germany after World War I. It was a cause of World War II.
   (5) ✗ UNREASONABLE The French and British were not eager for a war. They did not have the money for a massive military build-up.

4. (1) ✔ LOGICAL This would be passing a law respecting an establishment of religion, which is expressly forbidden in the amendment.
   (2) ✗ NOT LOGICAL Peaceable assembly is protected by the amendment.
   (3) ✗ POOR ASSUMPTION Just because the church is in Washington, D.C., does not mean that it is an agent of the government. Free exercise of religion is protected.
   (4) ✗ NOT LOGICAL Freedom of the press (newspapers, television, other media) is protected by the amendment.
   (5) ✗ UNREASONABLE While the amendment does not specifically say "Supreme Court," it does give permission to petition the government.

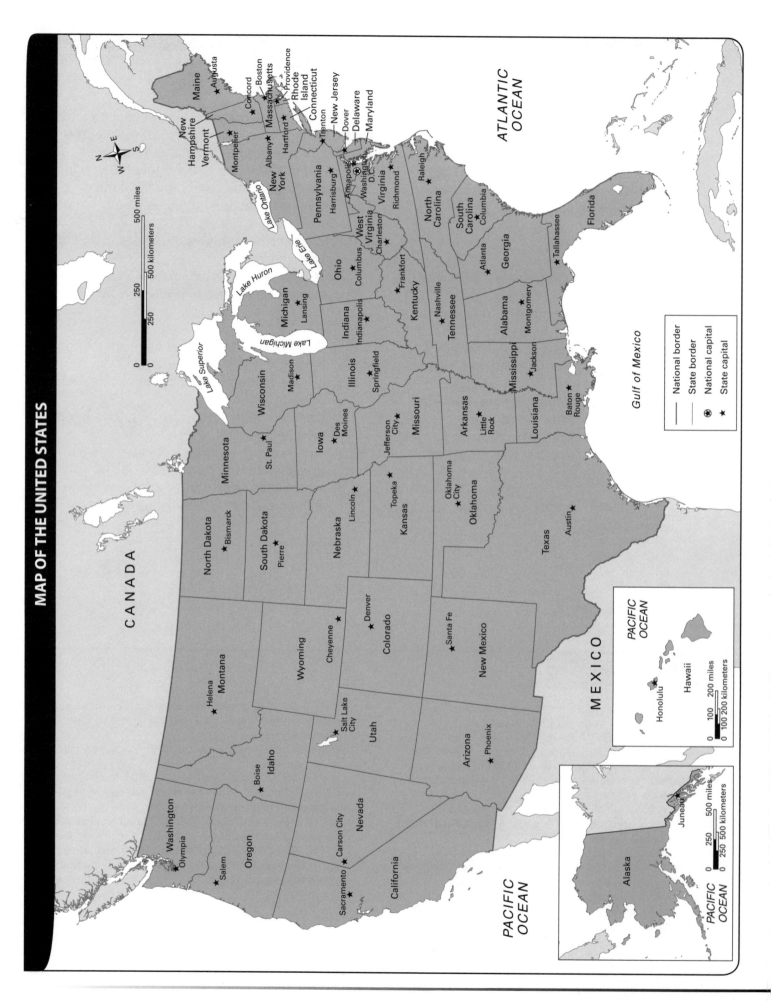

MAP OF THE WESTERN HEMISPHERE

GREENLAND
(DENMARK)

Hudson
Bay

Labrador
Sea

CANADA

Great
Lakes

UNITED STATES

ATLANTIC OCEAN

Gulf of Mexico

MEXICO

CUBA

HAITI

DOMINICAN
REPUBLIC

U.S. VIRGIN ISLANDS

BELIZE

JAMAICA

HONDURAS

ST. KITTS
AND NEVIS

ST. LUCIA

GUATEMALA

NICARAGUA

BARBADOS

EL SALVADOR

GRENADA

COSTA RICA

VENEZUELA

GUYANA
SURINAME

PANAMA

FRENCH GUIANA
(FRANCE)

COLOMBIA

PACIFIC OCEAN

ECUADOR

PERU

BRAZIL

BOLIVIA

PARAGUAY

N
W E
S

CHILE

URUGUAY

ARGENTINA

0   500   1,000 miles

0   500 1,000 kilometers

—— National border

FALKLAND ISLANDS
(U.K.)

ANTARCTICA

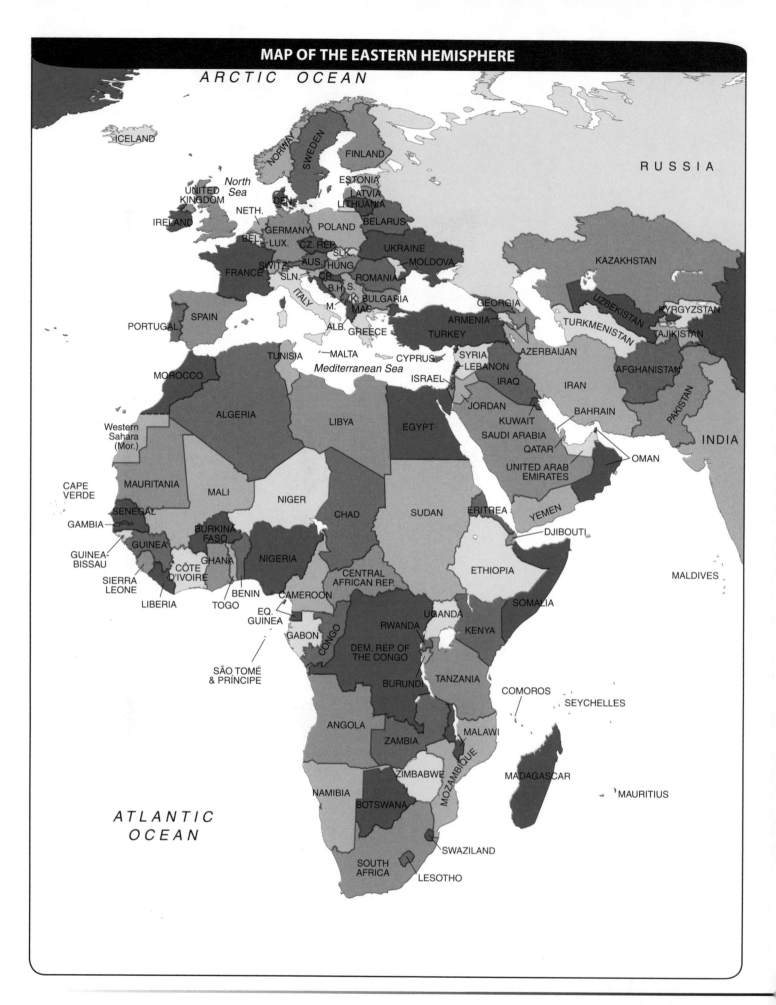

MAP OF THE EASTERN HEMISPHERE

ARCTIC OCEAN

Abbreviations

ALB.	ALBANIA
AUS.	AUSTRIA
BEL.	BELGIUM
B.H.	BOSNIA AND HERZEGOVINA
CR.	CROATIA
CZ. REP.	CZECH REPUBLIC
DEN.	DENMARK
MAC.	MACEDONIA
HUNG.	HUNGARY
K.	KOSOVO
LUX.	LUXEMBOURG
M.	MONTENEGRO
NETH.	NETHERLANDS
S.	SERBIA
SLK.	SLOVAKIA
SLN.	SLOVENIA
SWITZ.	SWITZERLAND

MONGOLIA

N. KOREA

S. KOREA

JAPAN

CHINA

BHUTAN

NEPAL

INDIA

BANGLADESH

MYANMAR (BURMA)

LAOS

VIETNAM

THAILAND

CAMBODIA

TAIWAN

PACIFIC OCEAN

PHILIPPINES

SRI LANKA

BRUNEI

MALAYSIA

SINGAPORE

INDONESIA

PALAU

FEDERATED STATES OF MICRONESIA

MARSHALL IS.

NAURU

PAPUA NEW GUINEA

SOLOMON IS.

EAST TIMOR

INDIAN OCEAN

N
W E
S

VANUATU

FIJI

National border

0 500 1,000 miles
0 500 1,000 kilometers

AUSTRALIA

NEW ZEALAND

GED JOURNEYS

JOHN DUTRA

John Dutra was almost too smart for his own good.
When John Dutra entered high school, he quickly skipped the ninth grade. Soon after, however, Dutra became bored with school and began to skip class. Eventually he left school to care for his mother and four siblings.

Dutra then enlisted in the United States Navy. Naval officers noticed Dutra's potential and encouraged him to attend the Navy Hospital Corpsman School, where he excelled. In 1954, with renewed confidence, Dutra decided to complete his high school education by taking and passing the GED Tests. As he recalled, "It was encouraging to me. It gave me a second chance. It paved the way for whatever achievements came later."

Dutra went on to earn undergraduate and graduate degrees from San Jose State University. In 1972, he founded Dutra Realty Enterprises, Inc. Dutra's understanding of geography and land-management led his company to grow to six offices, 250 agents, and annual sales of more than $900 million.

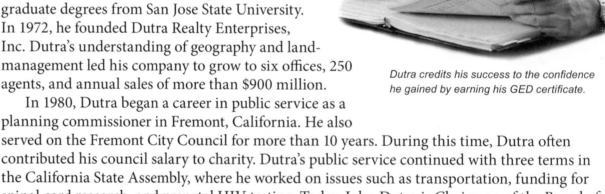

Dutra credits his success to the confidence he gained by earning his GED certificate.

In 1980, Dutra began a career in public service as a planning commissioner in Fremont, California. He also served on the Fremont City Council for more than 10 years. During this time, Dutra often contributed his council salary to charity. Dutra's public service continued with three terms in the California State Assembly, where he worked on issues such as transportation, funding for spinal cord research, and prenatal HIV testing. Today, John Dutra is Chairman of the Board of Dutra Enterprises, Inc., which specializes in land sales and development.

BIO BLAST: John Dutra

- Left high school to support his mother and siblings
- Served in the Navy and used the G.I. Bill to earn bachelor's and master's degrees
- Founded Dutra Realty Enterprises, Inc., which grew to annual sales of more than $900 million
- Served on Fremont Planning Commission, Fremont City Council, and three terms in the California State Assembly
- Awarded the Cornelius P. Turner award in 2004, given to a GED graduate who has made outstanding contributions to society

Geography

Unit 1: Geography

Whenever you hop on a highway, plan a vacation, or go hiking through the hills, you use geography to find your way. On a larger scale, geography allows us to determine our physical location and helps us understand how that location affects our everyday lives.

Similarly, geography plays a vital role in the GED Social Studies Test, comprising 15 percent of all questions. As with other areas of the GED Tests, geography questions will test your ability to interpret various types of maps and to answer questions about them through the use of thinking skills such as comprehension, application, analysis, and evaluation. In Unit 1, the introduction of essential map-reading and analysis skills will help you prepare for the GED Social Studies Test. For extra support, maps of the United States, the Western Hemisphere, and the Eastern Hemisphere are located on pages xiv–xvii in the frontmatter.

KEY GEOGRAPHIC TERMS

LESSON 1
Geography: the study of Earth
Globe: a model of Earth
Map: a visual representation of a place, usually shown on a flat surface
Equator: an imaginary line that runs around the middle of Earth, separating it into the Northern and Southern Hemispheres
LESSON 2
Scale: a map component used to measure distances
Lines of longitude: imaginary lines running north-south on a globe or a map in equal distances from one another used to find exact, or absolute, locations
Lines of latitude: imaginary lines running east-west on a globe or a map in equal distances from one another used to find exact, or absolute, locations
Key: an area on a globe or a map that explains the meaning of colors or symbols

Symbols: dots, stars, lines, arrows, or icons used on globes or maps to indicate cities, capitals, movement, or battles; explained in the map key
Compass rose: a symbol on a globe or a map used to indicate north, south, east, and west
LESSON 3
Physical map: a map that shows land and water features of an area such as mountains, plains, rivers, gulfs, and oceans; physical maps may also show climate (such as temperature) and elevation
LESSON 4
Political map: a map that shows how humans have divided the surface of Earth into states, countries, regions, or continents; political maps usually show borders and may also show roads or population data
LESSON 5
Special-purpose map: a map used for a purpose other than showing physical or political features; examples include tourist maps, battle maps, product maps, and congressional district maps

Table of Contents

Understand Geography

1 Learn the Skill

Geography is more than just the study of maps. **Geography** is the study of Earth. In Social Studies, the focus is typically on cultural geography—the impact of human culture on Earth and how humans are impacted by their geographical surroundings.

To understand geography, it is important to know some key geographic terms. A **globe** is a model of Earth, while a **map** is a visual representation of a place that is usually shown on a flat surface. The three main types of maps are physical maps, political maps, and special-purpose maps. The **equator** is an imaginary line that runs around the middle of Earth.

2 Practice the Skill

By mastering the skill of understanding geography, you will improve your study and test-taking skills, especially as they relate to the GED Social Studies Test. Study the map and strategies below. Then answer the question that follows.

A When reading a selection about geography, pay close attention to key geographic terms that may appear.

B Even though the countries on the map are not labeled, you can use their shape to determine their names.

The equator runs through fourteen countries spread over three continents. While it may seem that those countries should be the hottest on Earth, factors such as altitude and rainy climates keep temperatures down.

THE EQUATOR

NORTH AMERICA
EUROPE
ASIA
ATLANTIC OCEAN
AFRICA
EQUATOR
SOUTH AMERICA
PACIFIC OCEAN
INDIAN OCEAN

USING LOGIC

Find the equator on the map, and then locate the continents that it crosses. Use logic and your knowledge of geography to eliminate countries that are not within those continents.

1. Which of the following countries is on the equator?

   (1) Brazil
   (2) Mexico
   (3) Saudi Arabia
   (4) South Africa
   (5) Italy

UNIT 1

Directions: Choose the <u>one best answer</u> to each question.

<u>Questions 2 through 4</u> refer to the following map and information.

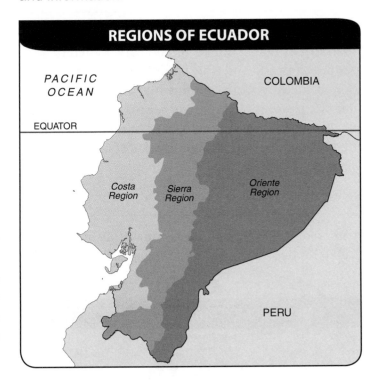

REGIONS OF ECUADOR

PACIFIC OCEAN

COLOMBIA

EQUATOR

Costa Region

Sierra Region

Oriente Region

PERU

Ecuador is located along the equator on the Western coast of South America. Ecuador has three geographic regions: the Costa, the Sierra, and the Oriente. The Costa runs between the coast and the Andes Mountains. The Sierra includes the Andes Mountains, and the Oriente to the east includes part of the Amazon Rainforest.

Most of the population of Ecuador lives in the Costa and Sierra regions. Many people migrated to the Costa region in the 1950s when banana production increased in that area. The Sierra experienced a similar population boom when oil was discovered in that region in the 1970s.

2. Based on the map and the information, why does Ecuador have different climates?

Ecuador's climates differ because

(1) it is on the equator
(2) most people live near the cities
(3) it has several types of geographic features
(4) the geography is the same throughout the country
(5) it is in South America

3. Why might Ecuadorians have migrated to the Costa region?

Ecuadorians might have migrated to the Costa region

(1) because they wanted to live in the Amazon
(2) because they wanted to live in the mountains
(3) because they could find jobs in the oil industry
(4) because the increase in banana production provided jobs
(5) because tourism jobs were available in the rainforest

4. Which statement best describes the Sierra region?

(1) it is located along the eastern border of Ecuador
(2) it is located along the west coast of Ecuador
(3) banana production caused a population boom
(4) it features the Amazon Rainforest
(5) it features the Andes Mountains

UNIT 1

Understand Map Components

① Learn the Skill

When you begin to analyze maps, you must first **understand map components.** Maps often include the following components: 1. **Scales** have small marks that stand for miles and kilometers. Scales help measure real distances on Earth. 2. **Lines of longitude** and **lines of latitude** are used to find exact, or absolute, locations of places. Lines of longitude run north-south, while lines of latitude run east-west. Relative location describes the position of a place in relation to other places. 3. **Symbols** such as dots for cities, stars for capital cities, or icons for special events, such as battles, can help you understand details on the map. Symbols are explained in the map key. Different types of maps use different symbols. Map titles, compass roses, and labels are also useful tools on a map.

② Practice the Skill

By mastering the skill of understanding map components, you will improve your study and test-taking skills, especially as they relate to the GED Social Studies Test. Analyze the map below. Then answer the question that follows.

A When you start to analyze a map, examine all of the components, such as the title and key. This will help you determine the purpose of the map.

B Use the scale to measure distances between cities.

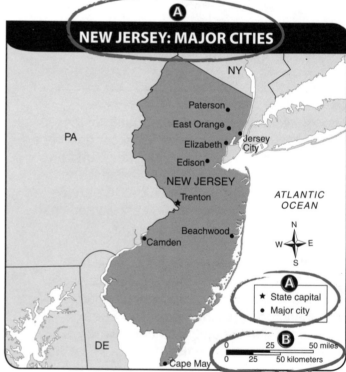

USING LOGIC

A compass rose is a multipurpose map symbol. It can help you find in what direction a city is located. It can also help you make generalizations about the relative locations of places.

1. Which area of New Jersey has the most major cities?

    (1) northwestern
    (2) western
    (3) southern
    (4) northeastern
    (5) southeastern

③ Apply the Skill

Directions: Choose the <u>one best answer</u> to each question.

<u>Questions 2 and 3</u> refer to the following map.

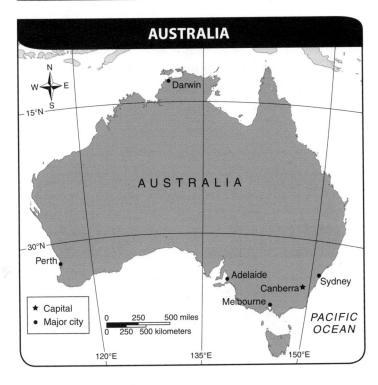

AUSTRALIA

2. Based on the map, which statement about Sydney is accurate?

   Sydney is

   (1) the capital of Australia
   (2) located on the west coast of Australia
   (3) north of Darwin
   (4) east of 150°E longitude
   (5) north of 30°N latitude

3. Based on the map, what can you assume about Australia?

   (1) most of the cities are located along the coast
   (2) most of the cities are located west of 120°E
   (3) most of the cities are located north of 15°N
   (4) most of the cities are located between 105°E and 120°E
   (5) most of the cities are located between 0 and 15°N

<u>Questions 4 through 6</u> refer to the following map.

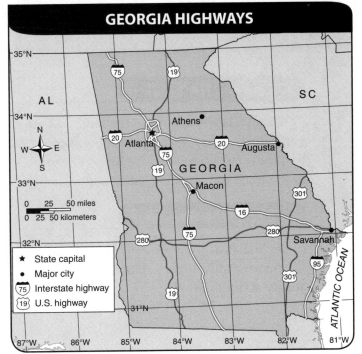

GEORGIA HIGHWAYS

4. Which interstate highway goes through Georgia's capital?

   (1) 19
   (2) 75
   (3) 95
   (4) 280
   (5) 301

5. Which city is near state highway 280 and interstate highway 16?

   (1) Athens
   (2) Atlanta
   (3) Augusta
   (4) Macon
   (5) Savannah

6. Which city's absolute location is closest to 81°W, 32°N?

   (1) Athens
   (2) Atlanta
   (3) Augusta
   (4) Macon
   (5) Savannah

Physical Maps

① Learn the Skill

A **physical map** shows the land and water features of an area such as mountains, plains, rivers, gulfs, and oceans. It can also show **climate** and **elevation**. Physical maps often use shading or different colors for elevation and climate, and symbols for cities and mountains, all of which may be identified in the map key. Social scientists can use physical maps to study settlement and migration patterns.

② Practice the Skill

By mastering the skill of analyzing physical maps, you will improve your study and test-taking skills, especially as they relate to the GED Social Studies Test. Study the map below. Then answer the question that follows.

A To identify a physical map, look for landforms and rivers.

B Use the key to learn about the meaning of the shading.

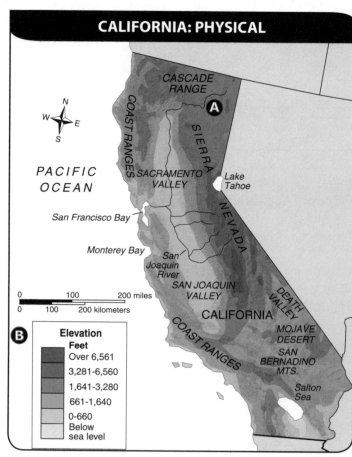

CALIFORNIA: PHYSICAL

B Elevation Feet
- Over 6,561
- 3,281-6,560
- 1,641-3,280
- 661-1,640
- 0-660
- Below sea level

MAKING ASSUMPTIONS

You might assume that physical maps do not show any boundaries, but they usually do. National borders are often shown on physical maps. State borders can also be shown. However, keep in mind that physical features can cross over state and national borders.

1. Based on the information in the map, which statement about the land in California is correct?

   (1) The land is a mixture of low land, hills, and mountains.
   (2) The land is mostly mountainous on the coast.
   (3) The land on the coast is very low.
   (4) The land in California is the same as the land in Nevada.
   (5) The land is mostly low with some hills.

Directions: Choose the one best answer to each question.

Questions 2 and 3 refer to the following map and information.

Michigan has over 11,000 lakes and ponds. Great Lakes Michigan, Huron, Erie, and Superior all border the state. Several of Michigan's more than 90 state parks are located near bodies of water, where visitors can swim, fish, and enjoy the natural beauty.

2. Based on the passage and the map, which statement about Michigan is accurate?

   Michigan

   (1) is south of Lake Erie
   (2) is home to the Muskingum River
   (3) surrounds Lake Huron
   (4) borders most of the Great Lakes
   (5) has only four state parks

3. Based on the map, which of the following is accurate?

   (1) Houghton is the name of a river.
   (2) Grand Lake is larger than Lake Erie.
   (3) Lake Michigan is east of Michigan state.
   (4) Silver Lake State Park is near Lake Michigan.
   (5) The Kalamazooo River flows into Lake Charlevoix.

Questions 4 and 5 refer to the following map.

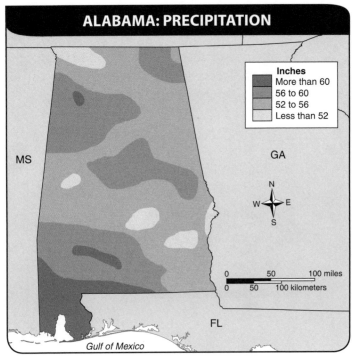

4. In general, where is the wettest area of Alabama?

   (1) in the east
   (2) in the north
   (3) on the coast
   (4) in the southeast
   (5) in the west

5. What is the least amount of precipitation that occurs along the Alabama/Florida border?

   (1) it is impossible to tell
   (2) less than 52 inches
   (3) 52 to 56 inches
   (4) 56 to 60 inches
   (5) More than 60 inches

Political Maps

1) Learn the Skill

A **political map** shows how humans have divided the surface of Earth. It shows **borders** between counties, states, territories, and countries. It can also show **human-made features** such as roads, buildings, and cities. Some political maps use shading or dots to illustrate areas where people live. This is known as **population density**. Areas with fewer dots or lighter shading generally are less populated.

2) Practice the Skill

By mastering the skill of understanding political maps, you will improve your study and test-taking skills, especially as they relate to the GED Social Studies Test. Study the map below. Then answer the question that follows.

A Political maps do not include physical features such as elevation, landforms, and rivers.

B Political maps show different levels of political borders including county and state borders.

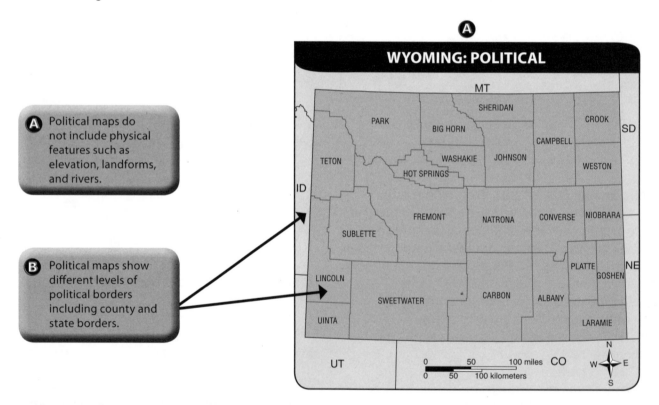

A

WYOMING: POLITICAL

TEST-TAKING TIPS

The map key changes for different types of maps. Some maps do not have a key. Be sure to study each map you evaluate to determine that map's features.

1. Which of the following is the best description of what this map shows?

    (1) the states that border Wyoming
    (2) the counties of Wyoming
    (3) the counties of Wyoming and the states that border Wyoming
    (4) the counties of Wyoming, elevation, and state borders
    (5) the counties and elevation of Wyoming

Directions: Choose the one best answer to each question.

Questions 2 and 3 refer to the following map.

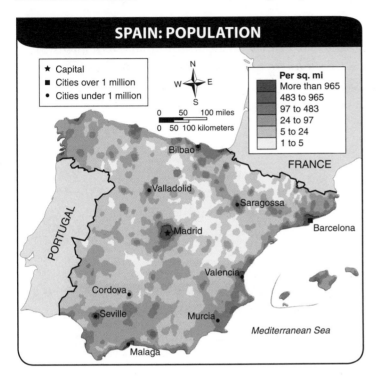

2. In which area of Spain is the population density the greatest?

   (1) between Madrid and Saragossa
   (2) along the Portuguese border
   (3) along the French border
   (4) between Madrid and Cordova
   (5) near most major cities

3. Based on the map, which statement about Spain is accurate?

   (1) Madrid has the highest population.
   (2) Seville is larger than Barcelona.
   (3) All areas of Spain have more than 10 people per square mile.
   (4) Few people live along the Mediterranean Coast.
   (5) Murcia has areas with more than 965 people per square mile.

Questions 4 and 5 refer to the following map.

4. What does the symbol next to Tucson probably represent?

   The symbol probably means

   (1) county seat
   (2) county seat and large city
   (3) state capital
   (4) state capital and county seat
   (5) large city and state capital

5. Based on the map, what can be assumed about Arizona?

   (1) Maricopa County has the largest population.
   (2) Coconino County has the largest population.
   (3) The state's population is evenly distributed across all counties.
   (4) Most of the population is near the California border.
   (5) There are no large cities in southern Arizona.

Movement on Maps

1 Learn the Skill

To understand **movement on maps**, it is important to know the symbols and map elements that are commonly used to show movement. Symbols such as **arrows** or **lines** can show the movement, direction, or route of people, goods, or ideas. **Colors** can also be used to show when movements occurred or to illustrate the forces or factors that caused the movement. Some maps that show movement are special-purpose maps. There is more information about special-purpose maps in Unit 4. Movement, or migration, is an important factor in understanding geography.

2 Practice the Skill

By mastering the skill of understanding movement on maps, you will improve your study and test-taking skills, especially as they relate to the GED Social Studies Test. Study the map below. Then answer the question that follows.

A Look at the arrows to understand the direction of the movements.

B When dealing with movement on maps, be sure to note the geographical areas involved. Which areas are the movements to, from, or between? What do you know about those areas during the time period specified on the map?

ATLANTIC SLAVE TRADE ROUTES

Map legend:
- ◄--- Slave traders' routes early 1500s
- ◄— Slave traders' routes 1600s
- ◄— Slave traders' routes after 1619
- Slave gathering areas
- Major concentration of slaves

NORTH AMERICA · Great Lakes · Mississippi R. · Gulf of Mexico · CUBA · HISPANIOLA · ATLANTIC OCEAN · EUROPE · AFRICA · SOUTH AMERICA · PACIFIC OCEAN

0   1,000   2,000 miles
0 1,000 2,000 kilometers

TEST-TAKING TIPS

Use the map key to determine the meaning of different colors on the map.

1. Jamestown Colony was founded in Virginia in 1609.

   What changes on this map after the founding of Jamestown?

   (1) The slave-gathering areas of Africa increase.
   (2) Areas with major concentrations of slaves move from South America to Africa.
   (3) More slaves are sent from South America.
   (4) The trade routes extend to North America in 1619.
   (5) The trade routes generally run west to east.

Directions: Choose the <u>one best answer</u> to each question.

<u>Questions 2 and 3</u> refer to the following information and map.

The Silk Road was not just one road. It was a series of ancient trade routes that stretched more than 4,000 miles from the East to the West. The main overland route, called the Silk Road, extended from China to the Mediterranean Sea.

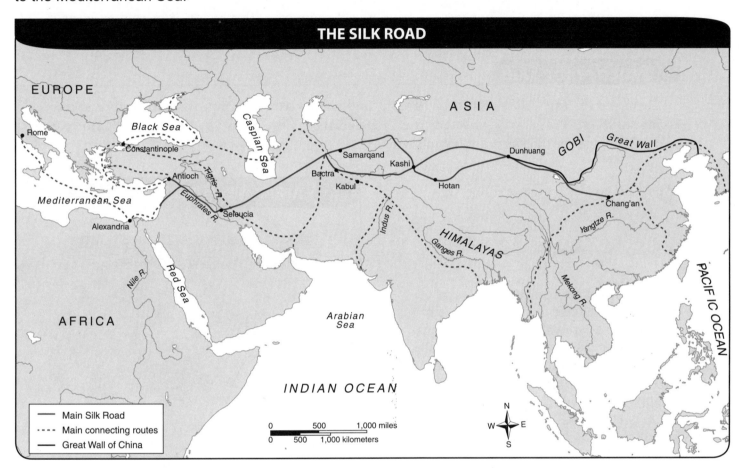

2. Why was the Silk Road important?

   (1) It boosted the economy of South America.
   (2) It proved that the world was round.
   (3) It provided silk to wealthy Asians.
   (4) It fostered the growth of the Dutch and English navies.
   (5) It allowed for goods and ideas to be exchanged between Asia and Europe.

3. How might goods from Alexandria have reached Kabul?

   Goods from Alexandria probably reached Kabul

   (1) via Rome and Constantinople
   (2) via Seleucia and Bactra
   (3) across the Mediterranean Sea
   (4) across the Great Wall of China
   (5) via Antioch and Samarqand

Relate Geography and History

① Learn the Skill

To understand how to **relate geography and history**, it is important to analyze the context of the physical, political, or special-purpose map and how it connects with a historical period or event. All of the map skills you have learned so far will help you make these connections.

② Practice the Skill

By mastering the skill of relating geography and history, you will improve your study and test-taking skills, especially as they relate to the GED Social Studies Test. Study the map and information below. Then answer the question that follows.

A Look at the time period being discussed. Both the map and passage give you a reference point.

A In 2004, violence and lack of food caused the number of displaced African refugees to soar over 2 million. Most of the refugees were concentrated in east-central African countries. **B** Tanzania had the largest refugee population. The United Nations believed that peace was returning to many areas and hoped to get donations to help defer the cost of sending the refugees back home.

B What details are mentioned in the passage that are not shown on the map?

AFRICAN REFUGEE AREAS: 2004

- Refugee area

MAKING ASSUMPTIONS

Note possible answers with the words *every, all, none,* or *never.* In social studies, few questions are so narrowly defined. You can almost always assume that answers that contain those words are not the best choices.

1. Based on the map and the information, which statement about Africa is true?

   (1) North Africa seemed to be the safest region.
   (2) The economy of Tanzania was affected by the refugees.
   (3) The United Nations paid for the care of the refugees.
   (4) Most of the violence took place in countries bordering Uganda.
   (5) In 2004, there was violence in every African country.

Directions: Choose the <u>one best answer</u> to each question.

Question 2 refers to the following map.

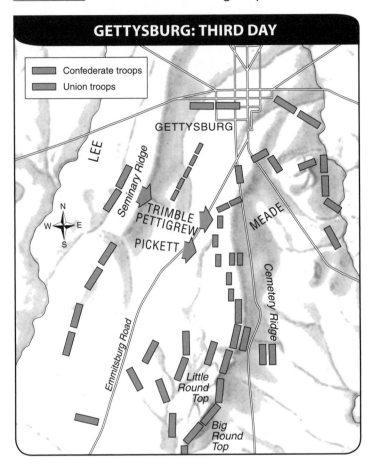

2. In 1863, the Confederacy lost the Battle of Gettysburg and retreated. Analyze the map. Which details show why this may have happened?

   On the third day of the battle, the Confederacy

   (1) held the town and had more troops
   (2) attacked Little Round Top
   (3) waited for the Union to cross the Emmitsburg Road and attack
   (4) advanced over open ground and their troops were stretched thin
   (5) focused on defending the town of Gettysburg

Question 3 refers to the following maps.

3. Which countries were most affected by World War I?

   (1) Austria-Hungary and Serbia
   (2) Germany and the Netherlands
   (3) the United Kingdom and Russia
   (4) Spain and Montenegro
   (5) Romania and Italy

Unit 1 Review

The Unit Review is structured to resemble the GED Social Studies Test. Be sure to read each question and all possible answers very carefully before choosing your answer.

To record your answers, fill in the numbered circle that corresponds to the answer you select for each question in the Unit Review.

Do not rest your pencil on the answer area while considering your answer. Make no stray or unnecessary marks. If you change an answer, erase your first mark completely.

Mark only one answer space for each question; multiple answers will be scored as incorrect.

Sample Question

How can historians use geography?

Historians use geography

(1) to learn locations
(2) to study how animals relate to their habitat
(3) to understand cultures in different areas of the world
(4) to figure out county divisions within states
(5) to determine which historical event happened as a result of another historical event

① ② ● ④ ⑤

Directions: Choose the one best answer to each question.

Questions 1 and 2 refer to the following map.

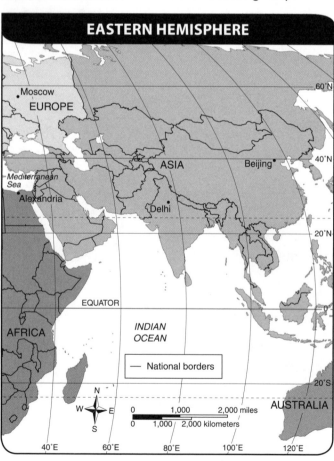

EASTERN HEMISPHERE

1. Based on the information on the map, what is the relative location of Beijing, China?

   (1) south of Alexandria
   (2) northeast of Delhi
   (3) 40N°, 80°E
   (4) 40S°, 80°W
   (5) west of Moscow

   ① ② ③ ④ ⑤

2. What tool could you use to find the absolute location of a place?

   (1) a scale
   (2) a key
   (3) relative location
   (4) map symbols
   (5) latitude and longitude

   ① ② ③ ④ ⑤

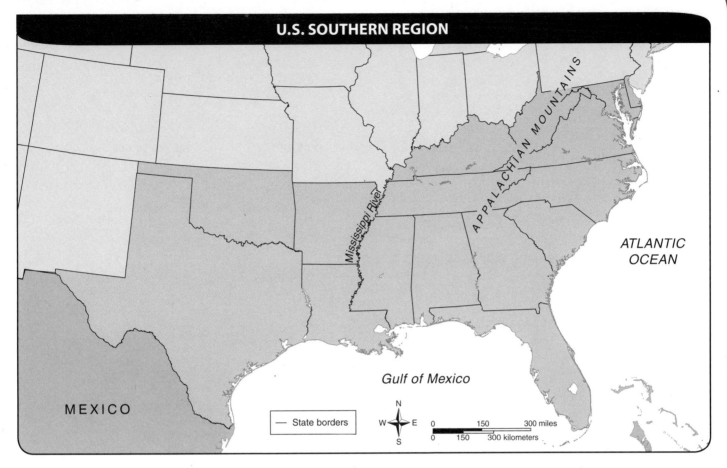

U.S. SOUTHERN REGION

APPALACHIAN MOUNTAINS

Mississippi River

ATLANTIC OCEAN

Gulf of Mexico

MEXICO

— State borders

N
W—E
S

| 0 | 150 | 300 miles |
| 0 | 150 | 300 kilometers |

3. Based on the map, which of the following statements is accurate?

The United States southern region

(1) includes all states east of the Mississippi River
(2) includes Virginia, but not West Virginia
(3) includes New Mexico
(4) includes all states that feature the Appalachian Mountains
(5) includes all states that border the Gulf of Mexico

① ② ③ ④ ⑤

4. Which city is in the U.S. southern region?

(1) Los Angeles
(2) Nashville
(3) Cincinnati
(4) Phoenix
(5) St. Louis

① ② ③ ④ ⑤

5. About how far away are east Texas and west South Carolina?

(1) about 300 miles
(2) about 500 miles
(3) about 700 miles
(4) about 900 miles
(5) about 1100 miles

① ② ③ ④ ⑤

Questions 6 through 9 refer to the following map.

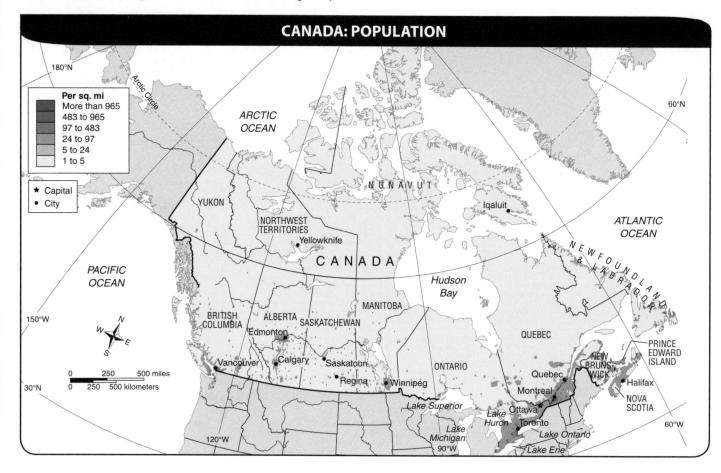

6. According to the map, where is most of the population of Canada located?

   Most of Canada's population

   (1) lives north of the Arctic Circle
   (2) lives between 60°N and 75°N
   (3) lives near Edmonton
   (4) lives near the capital
   (5) lives west of 120°W

   ① ② ③ ④ ⑤

7. Based on the map, which of the following provinces or territories probably has the highest total income?

   (1) British Columbia
   (2) Manitoba
   (3) Northwest Territories
   (4) Saskatchewan
   (5) Alberta

   ① ② ③ ④ ⑤

8. Based on the map, which statement best describes Canada?

   (1) There is plenty of quality farmland near the Arctic Circle.
   (2) Fishing and shipping have always been important to Canada.
   (3) Many Canadians have settled on the country's west coast.
   (4) Canadians do not value their relationship with the United States.
   (5) Hudson Bay is at the center of Canada's economic power.

   ① ② ③ ④ ⑤

9. Which city is closest to 60°N, 120°W?

   (1) Yellowknife
   (2) Edmonton
   (3) Calgary
   (4) Halifax
   (5) Iqaluit

   ① ② ③ ④ ⑤

Questions 10 through 13 refer to the following map and information.

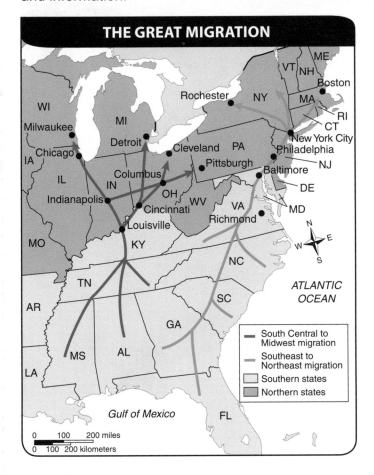

THE GREAT MIGRATION

Map legend:
— South Central to Midwest migration
— Southeast to Northeast migration
☐ Southern states
▨ Northern states

0 100 200 miles
0 100 200 kilometers

In the early 1900s, more than 1 million African Americans, pushed by discrimination and poor economic conditions in the rural south, migrated north and west in an event that became known as the Great Migration. The migration began around 1916, lessened during the Great Depression, and increased again during World War II and after. Northern cities such as New York, Chicago, Cleveland, and Detroit saw the greatest African American population increases. Manufacturing and other urban jobs led African Americans to these cities. Moving to cities also caused a growth in African American literacy and an African American cultural explosion. Many southern African American artists, authors, and musicians converged on New York City because it was seen as a cultural center of the United States.

10. Where were African Americans from Georgia most likely to have migrated?

(1) South Carolina
(2) Ohio
(3) West Virginia
(4) Illinois
(5) New York

①②③④⑤

11. Which of the following factors contributed to the Great Migration?

(1) the Great Depression and an increase in rural jobs
(2) World War II and an increase in southern factory jobs
(3) World War I and Jim Crow laws
(4) crop failure and lack of jobs in Detroit
(5) the boll weevil and poor living conditions in cities

①②③④⑤

12. Which of the following was a result of the Great Migration?

(1) World War I
(2) World War II
(3) Jim Crow laws
(4) the Harlem Renaissance
(5) the Great Depression

①②③④⑤

13. How was the United States affected by the Great Migration?

(1) increased urban workforce
(2) increased rural workforce
(3) decreased literacy
(4) decreased crop failures
(5) there were no lasting effects

①②③④⑤

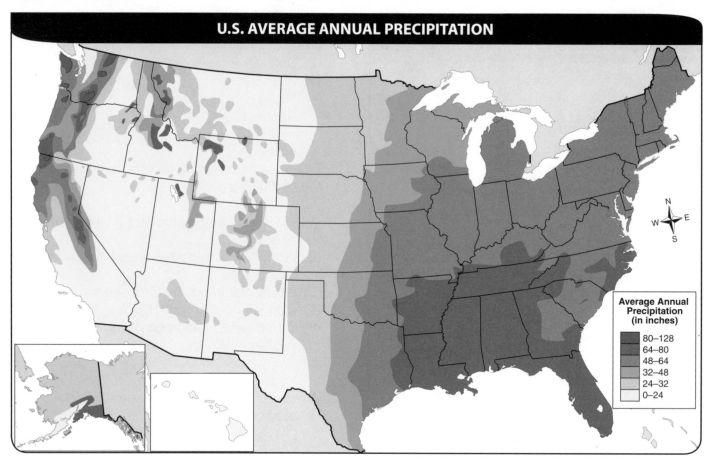

U.S. AVERAGE ANNUAL PRECIPITATION

Average Annual
Precipitation
(in inches)

80–128
64–80
48–64
32–48
24–32
0–24

Even though the United States is a large country, it features many different types of climates. The average annual precipitation, or rainfall, is one way to view those differences.

14. What state has the lowest annual precipitation?

(1) Washington
(2) Nevada
(3) Florida
(4) Texas
(5) Iowa

①②③④⑤

15. Based on the map, which area of the United States probably has the most diverse climate?

(1) the midwest
(2) the Atlantic Coast
(3) the Pacific Coast
(4) the southwest
(5) the northeast

①②③④⑤

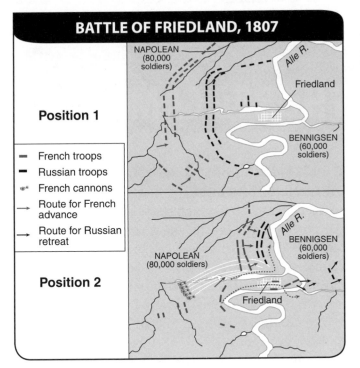

BATTLE OF FRIEDLAND, 1807

Position 1

- French troops
- Russian troops
- French cannons
- Route for French advance
- Route for Russian retreat

Position 2

OHIO: EARLY SETTLEMENT

(1789) Date city was founded
Rivers

Napoleon's victory over Russia at the Battle of Friedland ended the Third Coalition of European countries' attempt to stop the Emperor from controlling the entire continent.

16. What advantages did the French have?

The French

(1) had cannons and more troops
(2) controlled Friedland and were led by Napoleon
(3) controlled the Alle River and had cannons
(4) had more troops and were led by Bennigsen
(5) controlled Friedland and were led by Bennigsen

① ② ③ ④ ⑤

17. How did geography help the French win?

(1) The Russians could transport troops using the Alle River.
(2) The Russians were trapped against the Alle River and could not retreat quickly.
(3) The French got bogged down in the creeks.
(4) The French were unable to place their cannons because of the terrain.
(5) The French controlled the high ground.

① ② ③ ④ ⑤

18. Based on the map, which of the following statements is accurate?

The settlements in the Ohio Country

(1) were near Pennsylvania so they could be protected
(2) were mostly along Lake Erie
(3) were not near any Native American populations
(4) were all built along waterways
(5) were mostly in the interior of the territory

① ② ③ ④ ⑤

19. Soon after which historical event were most of the settlements in the Ohio Country founded?

(1) the American Revolution
(2) World War I
(3) the French and Indian War
(4) the War of 1812
(5) the Iroquois wars

① ② ③ ④ ⑤

Unit 2

BEN NIGHTHORSE CAMPBELL

Earning his GED certificate opened the door to a world of possibilities for Campbell.

The odds were against Ben Nighthorse Campbell, but he beat them anyway. As a teenager, Campbell left high school to join the United States Air Force. While enlisted, he earned his GED certificate. In 1957, after his service commitment, Campbell attended and graduated from San Jose State University, with degrees in physical education and fine arts.

In 1960, Campbell went to Tokyo, Japan, to attend Meiji University and study judo. Four years later, he captained the U.S. Olympic Judo Team. Campbell later married and moved with his family to Colorado, where he trained horses and designed jewelry.

Campbell was elected to the Colorado State Legislature in 1982 and to the United States Congress in 1986. When Campbell was elected to the United States Senate in 1992, he became the first Senator of Native American descent in more than 60 years. As he notes,

> **I think what it takes to succeed is the ability to withstand and not give up, to keep trying—perseverance.**

While in office, Campbell remained close to his Native American heritage. As a member of the Senate Committee on Indian Affairs, he helped pass legislation to create the National Museum of the American Indian at the Smithsonian Institution. Today, Campbell works as a senior policy advisor with the law firm Holland and Knight, LLP.

BIO BLAST: Ben Nighthorse Campbell

- Born April 3, 1933, in Auburn, California
- Served in the U.S. Air Force during the Korean War
- Earned the 2008 Ellis Island Medal of Honor
- Represented the United States in the 1964 Olympics in Judo competition
- Served as a United States Representative and a United States Senator

Unit 2: U.S. History

In November 2008, Barack Obama was elected the 44th President of the United States. The landmark nature of Obama's election as our nation's first African-American commander-in-chief was significant because of the history of race relations in the United States. Less than 150 years ago, African-Americans were not allowed to vote, let alone hold office. Less than 50 years ago, U.S. students of different skin colors were forced to attend separate schools. Today, though, all that has changed. Whether in race relations or a host of other areas, it is important that, as United States citizens, we safeguard our country's future. To do that, we first must understand its—and our—past.

The importance of understanding U.S. history extends to the GED Social Studies Test, where it comprises 25 percent of all questions. As with other areas of the GED Tests, U.S. history questions will test your ability to interpret text and visuals, such as tables, charts, graphs, and political cartoons, through the use of thinking skills such as comprehension, application, analysis, and evaluation. In Unit 2, the introduction of core reading and thinking skills will help you prepare for the GED Social Studies Test.

Table of Contents

Interpret Tables

① Learn the Skill

One way to present facts, statistics, and other details in a clear, well-organized manner is to use a **table**. Tables allow authors to visually present information that might be too lengthy or complex to describe in a narrative passage.

Tables organize information into **rows** and **columns**. Rows run across the table from left to right. Columns run up and down the table from top to bottom. A monthly calendar is a good example of a table. Reading the title of a table, as well as the headings for its rows and columns, can help you interpret and use the information presented in the table.

② Practice the Skill

By mastering the skill of interpreting tables, you will improve your study and test-taking skills, especially as they relate to the GED Social Studies Test. Examine the table and strategies below. Then answer the question that follows.

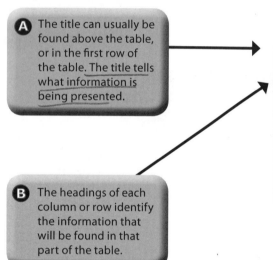

A The title can usually be found above the table, or in the first row of the table. The title tells what information is being presented.

B The headings of each column or row identify the information that will be found in that part of the table.

A

COLONIAL REGIONS	
REGION	**COLONIES**
New England	Massachusetts, New Hampshire, Connecticut, Rhode Island
Middle Colonies	New York, New Jersey, Pennsylvania, Delaware
Southern Colonies	Maryland, Virginia, North Carolina, South Carolina, Georgia

✔ TEST-TAKING TIPS

Use the headings of the rows and columns of a table in order to determine how the information in these parts of the table relates to each other. In this table, you can see that the region named in each row is related to the colonies listed to the right.

1. Based on the table, which statement best describes the New England colonies?

The New England colonies

(1) included all colonies north of Virginia
(2) included Connecticut and New Hampshire
(3) had the highest number of colonies
(4) were the largest group geographically
(5) were the only colonies founded by people from England

Directions: Choose the one best answer to each question.

Questions 2 and 3 refer to the following table.

POPULATION OF COLONIES, 1750	
COLONY	POPULATION
Connecticut	111,300
Delaware	28,700
Georgia	5,200
Maryland	141,100
Massachusetts	188,000
New Hampshire	27,500
New Jersey	71,400
New York	76,700
North Carolina	73,000
Pennsylvania	119,700
Rhode Island	33,200
South Carolina	64,000
Virginia	231,000

2. The information presented in the table supports which of the following statements?

   (1) Most of the colonies had populations of more than 100,000 people.
   (2) New York had a larger population than Delaware.
   (3) Rhode Island had the smallest population of any colony.
   (4) The population of Massachusetts was more than twice that of Maryland.
   (5) Pennsylvania was the second largest colony.

3. Based on the table, which statement best describes the colonial American population?

   (1) The colonies that covered the smallest geographic areas also had the smallest populations.
   (2) The Southern Colonies had the largest populations of any colonies.
   (3) Each region featured one populous colony and several other much more sparse colonies.
   (4) The earliest colonies most likely had larger populations than those colonies established closer to 1750.
   (5) The relative sizes of colonial populations would change very little after 1750.

Question 4 refers to the following table.

ESTIMATED POPULATION OF VIRGINIA COLONY	
YEAR	POPULATION
1650	18,700
1700	58,600
1750	231,000

4. The details in the table support which of the following assumptions?

   (1) Many people left Virginia to settle in other colonies between 1700 and 1750.
   (2) Virginia's colonial population peaked before 1750.
   (3) Daily life for Virginia colonists became more difficult over time.
   (4) Virginia had one of the smallest colonial populations in 1750.
   (5) Between 1700 and 1750, Virginia's agricultural economy diversified.

Main Idea and Details

① Learn the Skill

The **main idea** is the most important point of a passage or a story. The main idea may come at the beginning, middle, or end of a passage. A main idea may be clearly stated or it may be implied. If it is implied, you must use reasoning and supporting details to determine the main idea. You usually find the main idea within the **topic sentence**, or the first or last sentence of a given paragraph.

Supporting details provide additional information or facts about the main idea. Such details include facts, statistics, explanations, and descriptions.

② Practice the Skill

By mastering the skill of identifying the main idea and supporting details, you will improve your study and test-taking skills, especially as they relate to the GED Social Studies Test. Read the excerpt and strategies below. Then answer the question that follows.

A The main idea expresses the key point of a passage or story. It usually can be found in the topic sentence.

B Supporting details usually follow and provide additional information about the main idea.

From Thomas Paine's *Common Sense* (1776):

"... The infant state of the Colonies, as it is called, so far from being against, is an argument in favour of independence. We are sufficiently numerous, and were we more so we might be less united. 'Tis a matter worthy of observation that the more a country is peopled, the smaller their armies are. In military numbers, the ancients far exceeded the moderns; and the reason is evident, for trade being the consequence of population, men became too much absorbed thereby to attend to anything else. Commerce diminishes the spirit both of patriotism and military defense. And history sufficiently informs us that the bravest achievements were always accomplished in the non-age of a nation. ..."

✓ TEST-TAKING TIPS

Identify supporting details by first finding the main idea and then locating the information related to the main idea. These likely are the supporting details.

1. Which detail supports the main idea that Paine believes the colonies should seek independence from Britain?

   (1) The colonies were united through their large populations.
   (2) Growing commerce would lead to increased feelings of independence.
   (3) The bravest achievements, such as independence, come in a nation's early years.
   (4) The colonies lacked a sizeable military presence with which to pursue independence.
   (5) Independence and trade are consequences of growing populations.

Directions: Choose the <u>one best answer</u> to each question.

Questions 2 and 3 refer to the following information and excerpt.

When war broke out between Britain and its colonies on April 19, 1775, few Americans wanted to break from Britain. Instead, most colonists only wanted to gain rights within the British Government. As the war continued, however, many Americans began to believe that they could gain such rights only by breaking completely from Britain. On April 12, 1776, North Carolina allowed its delegates to vote for independence. A month later, Virginia delegates did the same. In June 1776, a committee including John Adams, Benjamin Franklin, and Thomas Jefferson met to prepare a document explaining the need for independence. That document was the Declaration of Independence.

From the Declaration of Independence:
"... We hold these truths to be self-evident, that all men are created equal, that they are endowed by their Creator with certain unalienable rights, that among these are life, liberty and the pursuit of happiness. That to secure these rights, governments are instituted among men, deriving their just powers from the consent of the governed. That whenever any form of government becomes destructive to these ends, it is the right of the people to alter or abolish it, and to institute new government, laying its foundation of such principles and organizing its powers in such form, as to them shall seem most likely to effect their safety and happiness. ..."

2. What is the main idea in this excerpt from the Declaration of Independence?

(1) All men are endowed with unalienable rights.
(2) Governments are responsible for the happiness of the people.
(3) People have the right to end destructive governments and form new ones.
(4) King George III of Britain was a tyrant.
(5) Life, liberty, and the pursuit of happiness are important freedoms.

3. The details in the paragraph and the excerpt support which of the following main ideas?

(1) After war broke out in 1775, the colonists wanted to be independent of Britain.
(2) Virginia and Thomas Jefferson led the movement for independence.
(3) Governments have a responsibility to secure liberty and happiness for its people.
(4) The colonists cautiously approached independence only after the British continued to violently oppress them.
(5) John Adams, Thomas Jefferson, and Benjamin Franklin believed that all men were created equal and with certain rights.

Question 4 refers to the following information.

A total of 56 men from all 13 colonies signed the Declaration of Independence. The signers ranged in age from 26 to 70 and included two future presidents, John Adams and Thomas Jefferson.

COLONIES	NUMBER OF SIGNERS
Connecticut	4
Delaware	3
Georgia	3
Maryland	4
Massachusetts	5
New Hampshire	3
New Jersey	5
New York	4
North Carolina	3
Pennsylvania	9
Rhode Island	2
South Carolina	4
Virginia	7

4. The details in the table support which of the following assumptions?

(1) Pennsylvania and Virginia were large and important colonies.
(2) Both signers who became president were from Massachusetts.
(3) North Carolina was smaller in size than Connecticut in 1776.
(4) Only two people in Rhode Island supported independence.
(5) The New England colonies supported independence more than the Southern colonies.

UNIT 2

Categorize

① Learn the Skill

A good way to organize information about people, places, dates, and events is to **categorize** it. To categorize means to place information in a group of similar or related items. For instance, when learning about a particular time period in history, you might categorize events into groups such as political events, military events, or economic events.

By sorting information into categories in this way, you can better examine how things are alike and different. Categorizing information can also help you understand patterns or trends throughout social studies. When you organize specific information into larger categories, it helps you see the big picture.

② Practice the Skill

By mastering the skill of categorizing, you will improve your study and test-taking skills, especially as they relate to the GED Social Studies Test. Examine the table and strategies below. Then answer the question that follows.

A The two main categories shown in this table are Federalists and Anti-Federalists. You can use the content of the table to determine whether other people or ideas should be categorized as Federalist or Anti-Federalist.

B Tables are useful tools for organizing the information that you categorize. Here, additional information about these groups has been categorized according to their views on government, views on the United States Constitution, and leaders.

FEDERALISTS AND ANTI-FEDERALISTS

GROUP	**B** VIEW ON GOVERNMENT	**B** VIEW ON CONSTITUTION	**B** LEADER
Federalist	Supported strong national government; wanted large military force; supported commerce and industry over agriculture	Supported adoption of Constitution	Alexander Hamilton
Anti-Federalists	Wanted to limit power of national government; believed states should keep as much power as possible; favored agriculture over commerce and industry	Opposed adoption of Constitution	Thomas Jefferson

USING LOGIC

When categorizing information, determine the most general categories into which your information can be grouped. From there, you can further group each set of information into more specific categories.

1. Which of the following statements could be categorized as expressing an Anti-Federalist viewpoint?

(1) Many small state militias should protect the nation.
(2) The Constitution should be ratified as quickly as possible.
(3) The national government must be capable of enforcing its own laws.
(4) The future of the nation depends upon the work of farmers throughout the nation.
(5) Taxes should be raised in order to support industrial growth.

Directions: Choose the one best answer to each question.

Questions 2 and 3 refer to the following excerpts.

From *The Federalist Papers: No. 2* by John Jay:

It has until lately been a received and uncontradicted opinion that the prosperity of the people of America depended on their continuing firmly united, and the wishes, prayers, and efforts of our best and wisest citizens have been constantly directed to that object. But politicians now appear, who insist that this opinion is erroneous, and that instead of looking for safety and happiness in union, we ought to seek it in a division of the States into distinct confederacies or sovereignties.

From *Anti-Federalist Letters from the Federal Farmer to the Republican:*

There are certain unalienable and fundamental rights, which in forming the social compact, ought to be explicitly ascertained and fixed—a free and enlightened people, in forming this compact, will not resign all their rights to those who govern, and they will fix limits to their legislators and rulers. …

2. Which two categories of individuals does John Jay identify in the first excerpt?

   (1) his supporters and supporters of Alexander Hamilton
   (2) people who believe in a strong central government and people who believe in a number of strong state governments
   (3) people who favor industry and people who favor agriculture
   (4) delegates who supported the Constitution and delegates who opposed the Constitution
   (5) supporters of state militias and supporters of a large national army

3. How might the author of the second excerpt have categorized the citizens of the United States?

   The author might have categorized citizens as

   (1) a group that is not free and enlightened
   (2) people who do not possess unalienable and fundamental rights
   (3) individuals who support a strong national government
   (4) a group that has resigned all of their rights to the government
   (5) people who want limited government

Questions 4 and 5 refer to the following information.

After the American Revolution, the states tried to expand their territory. In 1785, Georgia established a claim to land in what is now present-day Alabama and Mississippi. Spain, who had first claimed the territory, ordered the Georgian settlers to leave. In 1789, land companies purchased more land from the Georgia legislature. This land had been also claimed by Spain.

4. Into which category is this information best placed?

   (1) economic history
   (2) national political history
   (3) international political history
   (4) military history
   (5) social history

5. Based on the information, into which category could the future states of Alabama and Mississippi be best placed?

   (1) slave states
   (2) Southern colonies
   (3) Spanish colonies
   (4) Federalist states
   (5) Anti-Federalist states

Sequence

1 Learn the Skill

When you **sequence** events, you place them in an order, most often chronologically (from earliest to latest). By understanding the order in which events occurred, you can examine how one event can lead into another to produce a certain outcome. The ability to sequence further enables you to recognize how a past event might affect a current event, which could lead to a future result. In this way, sequencing events can help you make predictions about future outcomes.

2 Practice the Skill

By mastering the skill of sequencing, you will improve your study and test-taking skills, especially as they relate to the GED Social Studies Test. Read the information and strategies below. Then answer the question that follows.

A The final event or outcome of a sequence of events is sometimes described at the beginning or end of a passage.

B Look for words such as *first, next, later, finally,* and so on, that provide clues about the order in which events occurred. Times and dates also provide hints that you can use when sequencing events.

A By the 1840s, only a very small number of Native Americans remained in the southern United States between the Atlantic Ocean and the Mississippi River. Much of the Native Americans' removal from this area occurred through a series of treaties and legislation encouraged by President Andrew Jackson. After taking office in 1829, Jackson spurred Congress to pass the Indian Removal Act of 1830. This allowed Jackson to offer Native Americans territory in the west in exchange for leaving their native lands in the east. He also signed many removal treaties that forced Native Americans off their homelands.

One such group, the Cherokee Nation, disputed government policies in Georgia that limited their freedoms. The Supreme Court decided in 1832 that Native American groups were not subject to state laws. **B** Later, Jackson negotiated his own removal treaty with a Cherokee chief. Congress approved the treaty in 1835. When many Cherokee resisted leaving their lands, Jackson ordered a military response. **B** Finally, in 1838, troops led the Cherokee to the Indian Territory along the Trail of Tears.

MAKING ASSUMPTIONS

When reading information about history, you can usually assume that it is written in chronological order. However, sometimes historians organize material by themes. For example, a World War II historian may describe European battles and then Pacific battles, even though they often took place at the same time.

1. Which of the following events occurred immediately after Jackson became president?

   (1) Jackson negotiated a removal treaty with the Cherokee.
   (2) Congress approved Jackson's removal treaty with the Cherokee.
   (3) Congress approved the Indian Removal Act of 1830.
   (4) The Cherokee Nation disputed government policies that limited their freedoms.
   (5) Troops led the Cherokee along the Trail of Tears.

UNIT 2

Directions: Choose the <u>one best answer</u> to each question.

Questions 2 and 3 refer to the following information.

The War of 1812 began after a long period of escalating tensions between Britain and the United States. Tensions grew when British forces disrupted American ships carrying goods to Europe. However, another important cause of the conflict proved to be Americans' desire for additional lands along the frontier. Many settlers suspected that the British supported Native Americans in their conflicts with settlers. After the Battle of Tippecanoe in 1811, settlers became especially eager to remove the British from the area.

WAR OF 1812

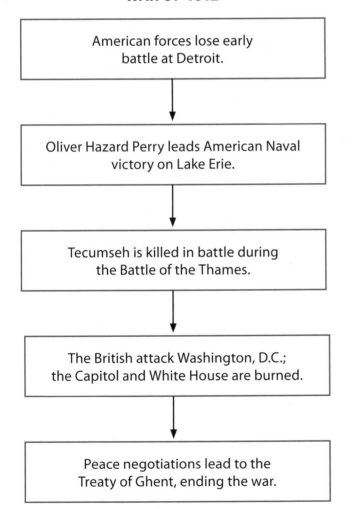

2. Which event preceded the War of 1812?

   (1) the Battle of the Thames
   (2) the British attack on Washington, D.C.
   (3) the signing of the Treaty of Ghent
   (4) the Battle of Tippecanoe
   (5) the Battle of Lake Erie

3. Which of the following events could be placed <u>last</u> on the sequence graphic organizer?

   (1) Support for the war in New England grew.
   (2) Britain ceded Canada to the United States.
   (3) The British defeated Andrew Jackson's forces at the Battle of New Orleans.
   (4) The United States became the most powerful nation in the world.
   (5) Nationalism began to grow in the United States.

Question 4 refers to the following information.

In the early 1800s, Texas was a part of northeastern Mexico. However, many American settlers started migrating to the area during this time. Texas gained its independence in 1821. However, the Mexican government insisted that Texans become Mexican citizens and convert to Catholicism. Texans also received orders to accept the Mexican government's ban on slavery in their territory. Texans largely disregarded these orders, and settlers continued to arrive. In 1835, about 30,000 Americans lived in Texas. When the Mexican government attempted to assert its power there, many American settlers revolted. This event became known as the Texas Revolution. The Texans gained a victory in 1836, and asked to join the United States.

4. When did Texas gain its independence?

   (1) before the United States gained its independence
   (2) during the same year that the population of Texas reached 30,000
   (3) more than 10 years before the Texas Revolution
   (4) after the settlers' victory in 1836
   (5) after joining the United States

Cause and Effect

① Learn the Skill

A **cause** is an action that makes another event happen. Sometimes causes will be directly stated in text. However, at times, authors may only imply the causes of certain events. An **effect** is something that happens as a result of a cause.

A single cause often produces more than one effect. On the other hand, multiple causes can work together to produce a single effect. By identifying causes and effects in social studies texts, you can better understand the connections between events and more fully comprehend what you have read.

② Practice the Skill

By mastering the skill of analyzing cause and effect, you will improve your study and test-taking skills, especially as they relate to the GED Social Studies Test. Read the information and strategies below. Then answer the question that follows.

A Here, the author of the passage directly states that one event has caused another.

B Other causes and effects are implied rather than explicitly described.

> During the Revolutionary era, northern and southern states had united behind the common goal of gaining independence from Britain. However, over time, differences between the two regions grew more pronounced. As the 1800s began, the South remained primarily agricultural. The Southern economy centered on plantations and the use of enslaved African laborers. The Northern economy, on the other hand, featured growing commercial and industrial sectors in addition to agriculture. **A** These differences caused economic and ideological friction between the two regions. **B** Disputes over states' rights emerged as questions arose about the legality of slavery in U.S. territories.

USING LOGIC

Look for key words and phrases such as *caused, affected, led to,* and *resulted from* that signal a cause-and-effect relationship. To confirm that you have correctly identified a cause-and-effect relationship, you should be able to logically restate the events as *A caused B.*

1. What is one effect of the sectional differences that emerged between the North and the South in the early- to mid-1800s?

   (1) The Northern states strongly supported states' rights.
   (2) Southern states urged the federal government to ban slavery in U.S. territories.
   (3) The South began using slave labor.
   (4) The Northern economy became increasingly diverse.
   (5) Northern farmers began establishing plantations.

Apply the Skill

Directions: Choose the one best answer to each question.

Questions 2 and 3 refer to the following table.

SOUTH CAROLINA POPULATION		
YEAR	WHITES	ENSLAVED AFRICAN AMERICANS
1790	140,178	108,895
1820	237,440	265,301
1840	259,084	335,314
1860	291,300	412,320

2. Which of the following would have most likely caused an increase in the enslaved African American population?

    (1) New fugitive slave laws were passed in 1850.
    (2) Many slaves escaped to the North along the routes of the Underground Railroad.
    (3) Agriculture remained the most common way of making a living in the South.
    (4) Northern abolitionists campaigned to end slavery in the South.
    (5) Most southern farmers worked on small farms.

3. Which of the following is the most likely effect of population data found in the table?

    (1) Northern abolition groups increased their membership.
    (2) Whites became increasingly nervous about possible violence from the enslaved African American population.
    (3) The slave trade ended because there was no longer a need for enslaved workers.
    (4) Enslaved African Americans had to find jobs in towns and cities because plantations had too many workers.
    (5) Whites gave the vote to African Americans so that South Carolina could have a greater representation in Washington, D.C.

Questions 4 and 5 refer to the following information.

Nat Turner was an enslaved person on a Virginia plantation. In 1831, Turner organized a group of fellow enslaved people and planned a revolt against their owners. With a group of about 60 people, he attacked slave owners in the surrounding area. Slave owners quickly retaliated. By the time the revolt ended, two days later, more than 50 people had lost their lives. Turner and his followers received harsh punishments and many of them were executed.

4. What was one probable effect of Nat Turner's revolt?

    Nat Turner's revolt most likely caused

    (1) slave owners to offer additional rights to enslaved people
    (2) Northern abolitionists to give up their efforts
    (3) additional slave revolts to break out across the South
    (4) slave owners to seek a diplomatic solution to the conflict
    (5) southern officials to develop more restrictive policies towards enslaved people

5. What might have caused Turner and his followers to plan their revolt?

    (1) anger over the harsh conditions under which they lived
    (2) disagreements over the meaning of the Emancipation Proclamation
    (3) a desire to share in the profits made by the plantations at which they worked
    (4) support for the leaders of the Underground Railroad
    (5) resentment at the passage of new fugitive slave laws

Compare and Contrast

1 Learn the Skill

When you **compare** two or more items, you consider both the similarities and differences between them. The study of history, geography, civics, and other social studies subjects often requires you to compare details about people, places, and events.

To **contrast** means to focus only on the differences between items. By focusing on the ways in which things are alike and different, you gain a deeper understanding of the material you read.

2 Practice the Skill

By mastering the skill of comparing and contrasting, you will improve your study and test-taking skills, especially as they relate to the GED Social Studies Test. Read the information and strategies below. Then answer the question that follows.

A You may find information to compare and contrast in both text and visuals, such as tables, charts, or graphs.

B Words and phrases such as *similarly, likewise, on the other hand,* and *however* often signal that an author is comparing or contrasting information.

As the Civil War came to a close, President Abraham Lincoln began to consider how the United States should be rebuilt. His plan for reconstructing the South called for generous terms that would allow the nation to heal with as little animosity between the North and the South as possible. On the other hand, radical Republicans in Congress strongly opposed this plan. They believed that the Confederacy should receive harsh penalties for the difficulties of the Civil War.

MAKING ASSUMPTIONS

You may assume that most parallel items described in a text or visual can be compared and contrasted. For instance, the text on this page compares and contrasts the Reconstruction plans of Abraham Lincoln and radical Republicans. Make sure, however, that the items you compare and contrast relate to each other in a similar way, such as two different plans or two different fruits.

1. When comparing or contrasting the plans of Lincoln and the radical Republicans, which of the following statements is accurate?

The Reconstruction plans of Lincoln and the radical Republicans

(1) both aimed to rebuild the nation as quickly as possible
(2) featured different objectives for the process of Reconstruction
(3) imposed similarly harsh penalties on the Confederacy
(4) featured different timetables for bringing the nation together
(5) delegated much of the responsibility for Reconstruction to state governments

Apply the Skill

Directions: Choose the one best answer to each question.

Questions 2 and 3 refer to the following table.

RECONSTRUCTION PLANS

LINCOLN	RADICAL REPUBLICANS
Aimed at reconciliation	Hoped to institute harsh punishments for Confederates
Offered pardons to former Confederates who agreed to support the Constitution and the United States	Refused to seat any former Confederates in Congress
Allowed southern states to elect former Confederates to Congress	Placed southern states under military rule
Allowed Confederate states to rejoin the Union if they established anti-slavery governments	Established Freedmen's Bureau to assist former slaves

2. How could you compare the plans of Lincoln and the radical Republicans?

   The Reconstruction plans of Lincoln and the radicals were similar in that they both

   (1) made rejoining the nation simple for former Confederate states
   (2) met with strong opposition in the South
   (3) hoped to successfully rebuild the United States
   (4) allowed former Confederates to participate in the rebuilding process
   (5) called for Northern officials to oversee the establishment of new governments

3. In contrast to the radical plan for Reconstruction, how is Lincoln's plan best described?

   (1) peace-making
   (2) punitive
   (3) bold
   (4) harsh
   (5) ambitious

Questions 4 and 5 refer to the following information.

In early June 1863, General Robert E. Lee led his Army of Northern Virginia into Pennsylvania. Lee's aim was to capture the railroad hub at Harrisburg, Pennsylvania, and force Union troops in Virginia to move north to engage him. While marching through the fields of Pennsylvania, Lee forbade his troops from looting the farms or destroying any homes. The Confederate troops "paid" for the food they took to support their army with useless Confederate money.

Nearly a year later in May 1864, Union General William T. Sherman began his march through Georgia to the sea. However, Sherman encouraged his men to take all of the food and livestock from the farms they passed. Sherman needed food because he was cut off from Union supplies. He also burned homes and barns. Sherman's aim was to demoralize the South and destroy any supplies that could be used to aid the Confederate Army.

4. How do Lee's actions contrast with those of Sherman?

   Lee

   (1) wanted to destroy the farms of the Pennsylvanians
   (2) wanted to fight a battle at Gettysburg
   (3) believed that Confederate citizens would follow him north
   (4) wanted to demoralize the South
   (5) believed that by being kind to Northerners the Confederacy might win their support

5. In what way were Lee's and Sherman's ultimate goals similar?

   (1) Both wanted to take food and livestock from farmers.
   (2) Both wanted to control new territories.
   (3) Both wanted to destroy the fighting spirit of the South.
   (4) Both wanted to find a way to end the war.
   (5) Both wanted to win a great victory.

UNIT 2

Interpret Charts and Graphs

① Learn the Skill

Charts and **graphs** are another way to present information visually. Like tables, charts and graphs can present a great deal of information in a relatively small amount of space. In social studies, authors often use these elements to show information that would be too lengthy to describe in a narrative passage. Charts and graphs also have the additional benefit of clearly showing change over time.

② Practice the Skill

By mastering the skill of interpreting charts and graphs, you will improve your study and test-taking skills, especially as they relate to the GED Social Studies Test. Examine the line graph and strategies below. Then answer the question that follows.

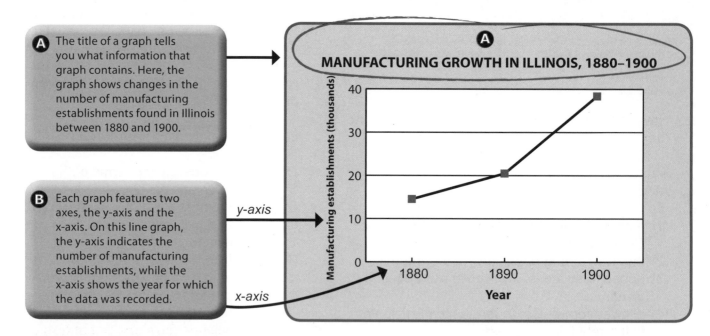

A The title of a graph tells you what information that graph contains. Here, the graph shows changes in the number of manufacturing establishments found in Illinois between 1880 and 1900.

B Each graph features two axes, the y-axis and the x-axis. On this line graph, the y-axis indicates the number of manufacturing establishments, while the x-axis shows the year for which the data was recorded.

MANUFACTURING GROWTH IN ILLINOIS, 1880–1900

USING LOGIC

To interpret a graph, refer to both axes and determine how they relate to one another at certain points on the graph. For instance, to determine the number of manufacturing establishments found in Illinois in 1890, you would scan up from the point on the x-axis for 1890 and find the number on the y-axis.

1. During the 1890s, what happened to the number of manufacturing establishments in Illinois?

   (1) They increased slightly.
   (2) They decreased slightly.
   (3) They remained nearly the same.
   (4) They increased dramatically.
   (5) They decreased dramatically.

Directions: Choose the one best answer to each question.

Questions 2 and 3 refer to the following bar graph.

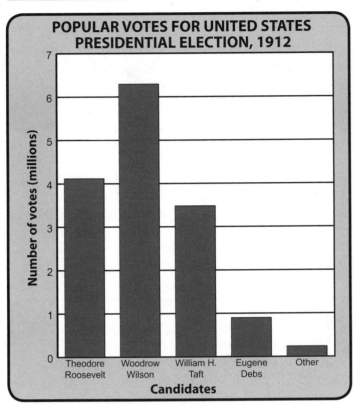

POPULAR VOTES FOR UNITED STATES PRESIDENTIAL ELECTION, 1912

Questions 4 and 5 refer to the following circle graphs.

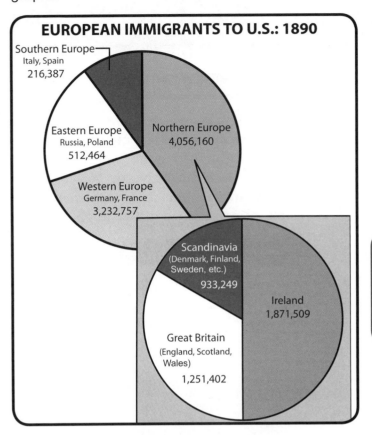

EUROPEAN IMMIGRANTS TO U.S.: 1890

Southern Europe
Italy, Spain
216,387

Eastern Europe
Russia, Poland
512,464

Northern Europe
4,056,160

Western Europe
Germany, France
3,232,757

Scandinavia
(Denmark, Finland, Sweden, etc.)
933,249

Ireland
1,871,509

Great Britain
(England, Scotland, Wales)
1,251,402

UNIT 2

2. Which statement best describes the results for William H. Taft?

   William H. Taft received

   (1) more popular votes than Theodore Roosevelt and Eugene Debs
   (2) the fourth highest number of popular votes
   (3) fewer popular votes than Other candidates
   (4) approximately 3.5 million popular votes
   (5) around 5 million fewer votes than Woodrow Wilson

3. Based on the information in the graph, which of the following statements is accurate?

   (1) The election of 1912 was a multi-party race.
   (2) Theodore Roosevelt became Vice-President.
   (3) William H. Taft was elected President.
   (4) Woodrow Wilson won the presidency in a overwhelming victory.
   (5) Eugene Debs received nearly 1 million Electoral College votes.

4. Based on the information in the graphs, which of the following statements is accurate?

   In 1890,

   (1) more immigrants came to the United States from Ireland than from any other country
   (2) it is likely that more immigrants to the United States came from Germany than from Russia
   (3) southern European countries, such as Italy and Spain, provided the majority of the immigrants
   (4) twice as many immigrants were from Northern Europe than were from Western Europe
   (5) more immigrants came from Asia and Africa than from Europe

5. Which historical event most likely caused the immigration rates in the second circle graph?

   (1) defeat of Irish Home Rule bill
   (2) war between Sweden and Norway
   (3) continued eviction of poor Irish farmers
   (4) increase in British factory jobs
   (5) World War I

Make Inferences

UNIT 2

① Learn the Skill

An **inference** is an educated guess based on facts or evidence. When you make an inference, you put two or more pieces of information together to determine what they might mean. In this way, making an inference is similar to putting together the pieces of a puzzle. Even before you have assembled the complete puzzle, you can begin to determine what it will look like. As you study historical information, making inferences will help you to better understand the connections between people, places, and events that might not initially seem to be related.

② Practice the Skill

By mastering the skill of making inferences, you will improve your study and test-taking skills, especially as they relate to the GED Social Studies Test. Read the information and strategies below. Then answer the question that follows.

A This sentence states Wilson's intentions about U.S. involvement in World War I. This fact can be combined with another to make an inference.

B This information can be combined with the information above to make an educated guess about the way the American public felt about the war.

After becoming President in 1913, Woodrow Wilson's first term was dominated by the outbreak of World War I in Europe. **A** Throughout his first term, Wilson sought for the United States to remain neutral. Tensions grew when German submarines attacked American ships. Britain also interfered with American ships in an attempt to blockade Germany. Despite these incidents, Wilson worked to keep the United States out of the war. **B** For his re-election campaign in 1916, Wilson ran under the slogan, "He kept us out of war." Wilson won the election and began his second term in 1917.

 USING LOGIC

When making inferences, be sure that your educated guesses can be logically supported by the facts available. Even though an inference is a guess, it should still be a guess that has a strong chance of turning out to be true.

1. What can you infer about the American public's feelings toward involvement in World War I during Wilson's first term?

   (1) Most Americans felt that the United States should support Britain's blockade.
   (2) Many Americans supported Wilson's policy of neutrality.
   (3) Americans were angered by Wilson's diplomatic approach to foreign policy.
   (4) Many Americans wanted Wilson to devote more time to domestic affairs.
   (5) Most Americans hoped for the United States to avenge the loss of U.S. ships.

③ Apply the Skill

Directions: Choose the <u>one best answer</u> to each question.

<u>Question 2</u> refers to the following information.

Beginning in the second half of the 1800s, many women in the United States worked to gain the right to vote. Organizations such as the National Woman Suffrage Association and the American Woman Suffrage Association worked to gain this right through a national constitutional amendment and individual state constitutional amendments. After a number of states granted suffrage, women began to use their new voting rights to once again push for a national amendment. The Nineteenth Amendment granted women throughout the United States the right to vote in 1920.

2. Susan B. Anthony (1820–1906) served as a leader in the National Woman Suffrage Association.

    Which of the following inferences can you make about Anthony?

    Susan B. Anthony

    (1) lived in one of the first states to grant women the right to vote
    (2) remained bitterly opposed to the leaders of the American Woman Suffrage Association
    (3) traveled and lectured on the importance of woman suffrage
    (4) opposed anti-slavery and temperance amendments
    (5) voted in the 1920 Presidential election

<u>Question 3</u> refers to the following table.

In 1917, the National Woman Suffrage Association published *The Blue Book* in an effort to dispute some objections to women having the right to vote.

THE SUFFRAGE DEBATE	
OBJECTION	**ANSWER TO THE OBJECTION**
It would double the ignorant vote.	Statistics show that more girls than boys are graduating from high school. Equal suffrage would increase the number of voters with more education.
Most women are against suffrage.	The organizations of women that support suffrage are much larger than those organizations that oppose suffrage.
Women are overburdened. Voting would stop them from caring for their families.	The act of voting takes very little time. Almost all women can find some time in their day to read newspapers or otherwise educate themselves on issues before voting.
Women are too emotional and sentimental and cannot be trusted with the ballot.	The authors of *The Blue Book* point out several instances of how men in government have made emotional and sentimental decisions about war and economic policy instead of relying on logic.

3. What can you infer about the authors of *The Blue Book*?

    (1) They were relatively uninformed about the issues.
    (2) They were extremely angry at the objections raised to women's suffrage.
    (3) Even though some of the objections were true, they still felt that women should vote.
    (4) They believed that violent protests were their only chance to secure the vote.
    (5) They believed in using a logical, methodical approach to win an argument.

Interpret Political Cartoons

① Learn the Skill

Political cartoons are drawings that are intended to make political or social statements. These cartoons usually reflect the opinions of the artists who draw them. These individuals, known as **political cartoonists**, often use humor or satire to make their points. They may also use a **caricature**, or an exaggerated representation of a thing or a person's physical features, to present their point of view. By interpreting political cartoons, you can gain valuable first-hand knowledge of the different ways that people viewed historical events during the time in which they were happening.

② Practice the Skill

By mastering the skill of interpreting political cartoons, you will improve your study and test-taking skills, especially as they relate to the GED Social Studies Test. Examine the cartoon and strategies below. Then answer the question that follows.

A Symbols often help convey meaning in political cartoons through the use of words and images, such as the axe blade (vote) chopping into the tree (saloon).

B Political cartoons often include labels or captions that identify items shown in the cartoon. These labels or captions may appear within a cartoon or in the space below it.

C The man to the right of the tree is a caricature of a politician. He is the one saying the words at the bottom of the cartoon.

The Prohibition Party formed in the late 1800s and worked for many years to outlaw the production, sale, and transportation of alcoholic beverages.

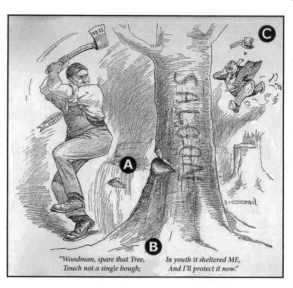

"Woodman, spare that Tree,   In youth it sheltered ME,
Touch not a single bough;   And I'll protect it now."

🧩 MAKING ASSUMPTIONS

You can assume that most political cartoons express some type of commentary or opinion from the cartoonist. As you examine the words, pictures, or symbols that make up a cartoon, think about how these items work together to express the cartoonist's views.

1. What do the depictions of the two figures in this cartoon suggest about the cartoonist's view on Prohibition?

   (1) The cartoonist believes that politicians are rightfully concerned about prohibition.
   (2) The cartoonist believes that the Prohibition Party is right in trying to outlaw alcohol.
   (3) The cartoonist fears that the Prohibition Party is pursuing their goals recklessly.
   (4) The cartoonist suggests that many politicians support the work of the Prohibition Party.
   (5) The cartoonist believes that the Prohibition Party is using illegal methods to achieve its goals.

Directions: Choose the one best answer to each question.

Questions 2 and 3 refer to the following political cartoon.

2. What do the figures standing along the outside of this cartoon represent?

   (1) nations about to begin fighting in World War I
   (2) groups competing for their own best interests in the League of Nations
   (3) groups opposed to the formation of the League of Nations
   (4) nations opposed to United States foreign policy in the early 1900s
   (5) countries hoping to form alliances with the United States

3. The cartoonist believes that the actions of the nations shown in the cartoon have negatively affected the world. Which of the following is accurate according to the cartoon?

   According to the cartoon, the actions of these parties have

   (1) harmed the United States economy
   (2) prompted the United States to take sides in disputes between other nations
   (3) led to the outbreak of new wars
   (4) prevented the United States from taking any action of its own regarding the League of Nations
   (5) forced the United States to quit the League of Nations and join the United Nations

Question 4 refers to the following political cartoon.

Following the stock market crash in 1929, President Herbert Hoover sought to minimize the effects of the crash on the U.S. economy. Part of his plan involved working with business and labor leaders to maintain wages and employment in the nation.

4. Which statement best describes the depiction of President Hoover?

   The cartoonist suggests that Hoover is

   (1) a weak and ineffective leader
   (2) guiding the country's economy back to stability
   (3) unsure of the correct course of action to improve the economy
   (4) making a mistake by supporting additional speculation in the stock market
   (5) wary of supporting big business during this crisis

Summarize

① Learn the Skill

To **summarize** means to briefly restate in your own words the main points of a passage or a visual element. When reading about historical events, you will often be presented with a great deal of detailed information. Through summarizing, you can determine which details are important and which are unimportant to understanding events and their relationship to one another.

② Practice the Skill

By mastering the skill of summarizing, you will improve your study and test-taking skills, especially as they relate to the GED Social Studies Test. Read the information and strategies below. Then answer the question that follows.

A When summarizing, leave out details that lack significance, or importance. Instead, concentrate on details that are important for understanding the main point of a passage.

B Look for the main points in a passage and think of ways to restate them in your own words.

> **A** Many scholars consider the launch of the first Soviet satellite, called *Sputnik,* in 1957 to be the beginning of the space race between the Soviet Union and the United States. **B** Striving for both scientific and political gain during the Cold War era, the two nations competed to achieve important milestones in space exploration. In 1961, President John F. Kennedy told the U.S. Congress of his goal of landing a man on the moon before the end of the decade. That declaration led to the creation of the Apollo program in the United States. The Soviet Union and the United States each wanted to become the first nation to place an astronaut on the moon. The United States won that part of the space race, landing astronauts on the moon with the Apollo 11 mission in 1969. Following this achievement, both nations began to scale back their space programs. As Cold War tensions gradually eased, a period of increased cooperation in space exploration between the two rival nations began.

USING LOGIC

Use logic to classify pieces of information as either main ideas or details. Think logically about whether each piece of information is the dominant theme of the passage or if it is a specific fact that supports a larger point.

1. Which of the following statements provides the best summary of the passage above?

   (1) President Kennedy was a leader of the U.S. space initiative.
   (2) The Soviet Union lost the space race to the United States.
   (3) The United States and the Soviet Union competed in a space race for scientific and political gains.
   (4) Apollo 11 was the first mission to place astronauts on the moon.
   (5) The space race slowed as Cold War tensions gradually eased.

UNIT 2

Directions: Choose the one best answer to each question.

Questions 2 and 3 refer to the following information.

Joseph McCarthy was elected to the United States Senate from Wisconsin in 1946. His early Senate career attracted little attention. However, McCarthy gained notoriety following a 1950 speech in which he claimed to have evidence of more than 200 Communist Party members working in the U.S. State Department. Soon, McCarthy became a powerful figure in the Republican Party. He was named the chair of the Permanent Subcommittee on Investigations. From this post, McCarthy held many hearings in which he accused numerous government officials of Communist ties. Over time, McCarthy's accusations became increasingly reckless and unpopular, even with members of his own party. His attacks on members of the U.S. Army proved especially divisive. McCarthy's investigations ended when the Senate censured him in December 1954.

2. A summary of this passage would likely include which type of information?

    (1) direct quotations from the passage
    (2) the names of some of the accused State Department officials
    (3) the dates of several of McCarthy's hearings
    (4) the circumstances surrounding McCarthy's election to the U.S. Senate
    (5) an overview of McCarthy's accusations and his eventual downfall

3. Which of the following statements best summarizes this passage?

    (1) McCarthy's accusations divided Republicans in the Senate.
    (2) McCarthy deserved to be censured by the Senate.
    (3) McCarthy correctly identified many Communist members in the State Department.
    (4) McCarthy gained power through his hearings on Communism, but then lost it with a series of unfounded accusations.
    (5) McCarthy became an important chair of the Permanent Subcommittee on Investigations.

Question 4 refers to the following information and map.

On June 25, 1950, North Korean forces crossed the 38th parallel into South Korea, marking the beginning of the Korean War. Within three days, the South Korean capital of Seoul had fallen. The United Nations advocated that its members send forces to help restore peace in the nation. By July 30, 1950, President Truman stated that he had authorized U.S. air, sea, and ground forces to assist South Korean forces in the conflict against North Korea.

4. What can you summarize about North Korea's invasion of South Korea?

    (1) North Korean forces quickly captured Seoul and Pusan.
    (2) United States forces quickly arrived at Seoul and recaptured the capital.
    (3) President Truman authorized various types of U.S. troops to aid South Korean forces.
    (4) Within five days of battle, the North Koreans reached the southern tip of the peninsula.
    (5) The South Koreans rejected the United Nations offer of assistance.

UNIT 2

Unit 2 Review

The Unit Review is structured to resemble the GED Social Studies Test. Be sure to read each question and all possible answers very carefully before choosing your answer.

To record your answers, fill in the numbered circle that corresponds to the answer you select for each question in the Unit Review.

Do not rest your pencil on the answer area while considering your answer. Make no stray or unnecessary marks. If you change an answer, erase your first mark completely.

Mark only one answer space for each question; multiple answers will be scored as incorrect.

Sample Question

What was the period of economic growth in the late 1800s known as?

(1) the Industrial Revolution
(2) the Golden Age
(3) the Civil War
(4) the Great Migration
(5) the Great Depression

Directions: Choose the one best answer to each question.

Question 1 refers to the following information.

Though woman suffrage workers had previously been divided in their course of action, by 1916, most suffragists had joined together to work towards a national constitutional amendment. Several events built momentum for the passage of this amendment. In 1917, the state of New York approved suffrage for women. The following year, President Woodrow Wilson offered his support for a constitutional amendment. The Nineteenth Amendment passed the House of Representatives on May 21, 1919. The Senate passed the amendment two weeks later. The amendment received the necessary support of three-quarters of all states on August 18, 1920, when Tennessee became the 36th state to ratify it. The amendment was officially enacted on August 26, 1920.

1. Which detail supports the idea that the suffrage movement had been divided before 1916?

   (1) Many Americans considered suffrage for women to be a radical change to the nation's Constitution.
   (2) Supporters of women's suffrage often met with harsh resistance during their campaigns.
   (3) The first suffrage amendment was introduced in Congress more than 40 years before the Nineteenth Amendment gained approval.
   (4) Some suffragists worked for suffrage acts in individual states, while others worked for a national constitutional amendment granting women the right to vote.
   (5) Suffragists often used strategies such as hunger strikes, vigils, and parades to promote their objectives.

   ① ② ③ ④ ⑤

Questions 2 and 3 refer to the following table.

U.S. PRESIDENTS SINCE 1960			
NAME	TERM	PARTY	STATE REPRESENTED
John F. Kennedy	1961–1963	Democrat	Massachusetts
Lyndon B. Johnson	1963–1969	Democrat	Texas
Richard M. Nixon	1969–1974	Republican	New York / California
Gerald R. Ford	1974–1977	Republican	Michigan
Jimmy Carter	1977–1981	Democrat	Georgia
Ronald Reagan	1981–1989	Republican	California
George H.W. Bush	1989–1993	Republican	Texas
Bill Clinton	1993–2001	Democrat	Arkansas
George W. Bush	2001–2009	Republican	Texas
Barack Obama	2009–	Democrat	Illinois

2. Who served as President between 1963 and 1969?

The President between 1963 and 1969 was

(1) Ronald Reagan
(2) Lyndon B. Johnson
(3) Richard M. Nixon
(4) Jimmy Carter
(5) George H.W. Bush

①②③④⑤

3. Based on the information in the table, which of the following statements is accurate?

(1) Candidates of the Republican Party dominated national politics during the 1960s.
(2) Most Presidents since 1960 have only served a single term in office.
(3) Only the Democratic Party had two of its candidates serve consecutive terms in office.
(4) Most Presidents since 1960 have represented states with large populations.
(5) Gerald Ford served the shortest term among these Presidents.

①②③④⑤

Questions 4 and 5 refer to the following map.

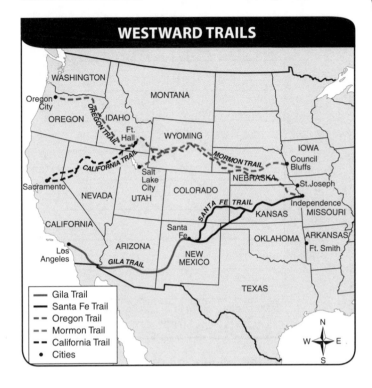

4. What is the main idea of this map?

(1) Settlers followed several different trails to reach the western United States.
(2) Independence marked the halfway point of the Oregon Trail.
(3) All trails to the west began in Independence, Missouri.
(4) Lewis and Clark took a more circuitous route to reach what is now Oregon.
(5) Settlers traveling west had to cross the Continental Divide during the journeys.

①②③④⑤

5. Which of the following details supports the main idea that settlers' journeys along the Oregon Trail were very dangerous?

(1) Very few settlers died from conflicts with Native Americans.
(2) Many settlers traveled west to escape economic difficulties in the east.
(3) Many Oregon Trail settlers traveled using prairie schooner wagons.
(4) Pioneers often had to discard supplies as their journeys progressed.
(5) Many settlers along the trail died from diseases such as cholera.

①②③④⑤

Questions 6 through 8 refer to the line graph.

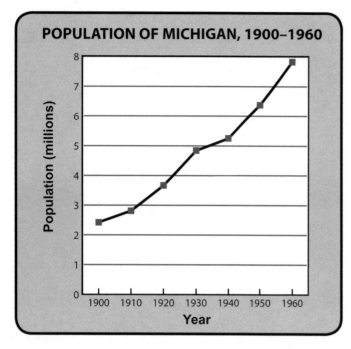

POPULATION OF MICHIGAN, 1900–1960

6. What was the population of Michigan in 1940?

   (1) slightly less than 5 million
   (2) less than 3 million
   (3) more than 6 million
   (4) approximately 5.25 million
   (5) approximately 3.75 million
   ①②③④⑤

7. During which decade did Michigan experience its greatest population growth?

   (1) 1900–1910
   (2) 1910–1920
   (3) 1920–1930
   (4) 1930–1940
   (5) 1950–1960
   ①②③④⑤

8. Based on the graph, which of the following trends is correct?

   Michigan's population

   (1) grew dramatically between 1900 and 1910
   (2) growth slowed after 1940
   (3) was affected by the automotive industry
   (4) grew at the same rate every decade
   (5) was affected by a growth in agricultural jobs
   ①②③④⑤

Questions 9 and 10 refer to the following information.

Following the Constitutional Convention, the leaders who supported the adoption of the Constitution became known as Federalists. Figures such as Alexander Hamilton, James Madison, and John Jay wrote in support of the Constitution. Federalists supported a strong national government. They also favored industries and big business. The Federalists became popular among wealthy merchants and Northern property owners. They also frequently supported the British in matters of foreign policy.

Thomas Jefferson led a group opposed to Federalist policies, called the Anti-Federalists. The Anti-Federalists, including James Monroe, opposed the adoption of the Constitution, favoring states' rights over a strong central government. The Anti-Federalists were also concerned about the Constitution's lack of protection for personal liberties. They gained support among Southern landholders and many less privileged citizens.

9. Why could James Monroe be categorized as an Anti-Federalist?

   James Monroe

   (1) was from Virginia
   (2) supported the Monroe Doctrine
   (3) served as President of the United States
   (4) supported the Virginia Declaration of Rights
   (5) negotiated the Louisiana Purchase
   ①②③④⑤

10. Which of the following statements could be categorized as describing a Federalist point of view?

   (1) Support for industry and trade should come before support for small farmers.
   (2) The United States should support the French in matters of foreign policy.
   (3) The states should refuse to ratify the United States Constitution.
   (4) The federal government should not restrict the rights of the individual states.
   (5) Citizens should support the presidential candidacy of James Monroe.
   ①②③④⑤

Questions 11 and 12 refer to the 1858 debate between Abraham Lincoln and Stephen Douglas.

Douglas: … Now, I hold that Illinois had a right to abolish and prohibit slavery as she did, and I hold that Kentucky has the same right to continue and protect slavery that Illinois had to abolish it. … that each and every State of this Union is a sovereign power, with the right to do as it pleases upon this question of slavery, and upon all its domestic institutions.

Lincoln: … I will say here, while upon this subject, that I have no purpose, directly or indirectly, to interfere with the institution of slavery in the States where it exists. … but … there is no reason in the world why the negro is not entitled to all the natural rights enumerated in the Declaration of Independence, the right to life, liberty, and the pursuit of happiness. I hold that he is as much entitled to those as the white man.

11. How are Douglas's and Lincoln's views on slavery similar?

(1) They both propose to make slavery illegal.
(2) Neither intends to interfere with slavery where it already exists.
(3) They both believe that states should have the right to decide whether slavery is illegal.
(4) They both believe that slavery does not restrict the natural rights of enslaved people.
(5) Neither believes that slavery will continue in the United States.

①②③④⑤

12. With what assertion of Douglas's would Lincoln disagree?

Lincoln would disagree with Douglas's assertion that

(1) slavery should still exist in the South
(2) the Declaration of Independence applies to all citizens
(3) the federal government has authority over state's rights
(4) each state has sovereign power
(5) African Americans should be able to vote

①②③④⑤

Questions 13 and 14 refer to the following political cartoon.

"BACKLASH,"
A 1966 Herblock Cartoon, © by The Herb Block Foundation

13. Who is the figure depicted on the left in this cartoon?

(1) Franklin D. Roosevelt
(2) Abraham Lincoln
(3) Lyndon B. Johnson
(4) George W. Bush
(5) Bill Clinton

①②③④⑤

14. What idea is the cartoonist trying to convey through this cartoon?

(1) The Great Society cannot help provide help for the war needs of the nation.
(2) Unlike the New Deal, the Great Society has not proven beneficial to the United States.
(3) Stopping the spread of Communism in the Vietnam War is more important than funding the programs of the Great Society.
(4) The President accidentally neglected the Great Society while tending to the Vietnam War.
(5) The costs of taking part in the Vietnam War would take away vital money from the Great Society programs.

①②③④⑤

In 1819, the United States included 22 states. These states were equally divided between those that allowed slavery and those that did not. However, when Missouri was poised to become the 23rd state, disagreements arose in Congress regarding whether the new state would be permitted to allow slavery. To solve this dispute, Congress reached what came to be known as the Missouri Compromise. This agreement allowed the northern part of Massachusetts to join the nation as the free state of Maine. In turn, Missouri would enter the nation as a slave state. This preserved the balance of free and slave states in the nation. Ultimately, the Missouri Compromise ensured that nine of the states created from the Louisiana Territory remained free.

15. What was the main cause of the Missouri Compromise?

The Missouri Compromise was ultimately caused by

(1) the disagreement over the borders of what would become the state of Missouri
(2) conflict between members of Congress regarding the balance of northern and southern states
(3) fears over the spread of slavery
(4) disputes over the control of valuable resources found in Missouri
(5) skirmishes along the borders between the North and the South

①②③④⑤

16. Which of the following effects of the Missouri Compromise is implied in the paragraph?

(1) Representation in the Senate would remain equal for free states and slave states.
(2) The plantation system would diminish in the South.
(3) Only free states would be admitted to the United States in the future.
(4) Hostilities broke out between Missouri and Maine.
(5) Missouri voters soon requested that slavery be made illegal in the new state.

①②③④⑤

The early portion of George W. Bush's first term in office was notable for his efforts to institute a program of tax cuts. He also strove to change or stop various policies that Bill Clinton had set forth in the final days of his term. Additionally, Bush proposed a number of measures designed to assist big business in the United States. His No Child Left Behind program instituted mandatory standardized testing for public schools throughout the nation. Bush's early foreign policy was dominated by the September 11, 2001 terrorist attacks and the United States' response to those attacks.

From the *Department of Homeland Security* June 2002:

"The President proposes to create a new Department of Homeland Security, the most significant transformation of the U.S. government in over half-century by largely transforming and realigning the current confusing patchwork of government activities into a single department whose primary mission is to protect our homeland. The creation of a Department of Homeland Security is one more key step in the President's national strategy for homeland security."

17. Based on the information above, what can be inferred about the Department of Homeland Security?

The Department of Homeland Security

(1) is not funded by federal tax revenue
(2) was created in response to the September 11, 2001 terrorist attacks
(3) was established to help big business in the United States
(4) was originally proposed by Bill Clinton during his final days in office
(5) is responsible for monitoring the standardized testing of public schools

①②③④⑤

Questions 18 through 20 refer to the following information.

THE TRANSCONTINENTAL RAILROAD

October 1861: Theodore Judah lobbies for federal funding of the Central Pacific Railroad Company.

↓

July 1862: The Pacific Railroad Bill authorizes the Central Pacific Railroad to build a railroad line from California. The bill also establishes the Union Pacific Railroad Company to construct a railroad westward from the Missouri River. The meeting of these will form the transcontinental railroad.

↓

January 1863: The Central Pacific breaks ground in Sacramento, California.

↓

December 1863: The Union Pacific breaks ground in Omaha, Nebraska.

↓

Late summer 1865: Central Pacific workers begin drilling 12 tunnels through the Sierra Nevadas by hand. Many Chinese immigrants contribute to this effort.

↓

October 1866: Union Pacific crews reach the 100th Meridian line. According to the Pacific Railroad Bill, this milestone allows the crews to continue building westward.

↓

August 1867: Central Pacific workers complete one of their greatest challenges by finishing the Summit Tunnel.

↓

April 1868: Union Pacific workers reach Sherman Summit in the Rocky Mountains, the highest point on either line.

↓

May 1871: The Central Pacific and Union Pacific meet. A golden spike is hammered into the ground to complete the transcontinental railroad.

18. Which of the following events occurred before 1867?

(1) Railroad leaders agree on the meeting point of the Central Pacific and Union Pacific.
(2) Union Pacific workers reach Sherman Summit.
(3) The Central Pacific and Union Pacific lines meet in Promontory Summit, Utah.
(4) Union Pacific crews reach the 100th Meridian line.
(5) Central Pacific crews complete work on the Summit Tunnel.

①②③④⑤

19. Which of the following events happened first?

(1) The Union Pacific breaks ground.
(2) The Central Pacific breaks ground.
(3) Central Pacific workers begin drilling tunnels through the Sierra Nevadas.
(4) Union Pacific workers reach Sherman Summit.
(5) The Pacific Railroad Bill is passed.

①②③④⑤

20. Which of the following events likely happened after the completion of the transcontinental railroad?

(1) Significant economic growth occurred along the railroad lines.
(2) Construction on competing transcontinental lines ceased.
(3) Population growth in the western United States slowed.
(4) Renewed tensions broke out between northern and southern states.
(5) The frontier remained free of settlers for many years.

①②③④⑤

GED JOURNEYS

JEANNE MARTIN CISSÉ

Jeanne Martin Cissé had a yearning to learn. Nearing age 80, a time at which most people ease into retirement, Cissé had other ideas—foremost among them earning a GED certificate.

More than a half-century earlier, Cissé had begun her career as a teacher in her native country of Guinea. In the years following, she became involved in politics, working on behalf of women and human rights.

Cissé went on to become the first woman appointed to the United Nations as a delegate. In 1972, she became the first woman to serve as president of the United Nations Security Council, a post she held until 1976. She also chaired the UN Special Committee against apartheid. She later served as an ambassador from Guinea to Brazil, Argentina, and Venezuela. She then worked as the Minister of Social Affairs in Guinea.

In addition to speaking five languages and becoming an American citizen, Cissé wanted to improve her English reading, writing, and speaking. She set—and met—the goal of earning her GED certificate before her 80th birthday. Cissé recalled her achievement as

" the best gift possible. "

In 2006, the GED Testing Service honored Cissé with its Lifetime Achievement Award.

GUINEA

Cissé addresses the UN Security Council in Panama City, Panama, approximately 30 years prior to earning her GED certificate.

BIO BLAST: Jeanne Martin Cissé

- Native of Guinea, where she began her career as a teacher
- First female delegate to the United Nations
- First woman to preside over the United Nations Security Council
- Speaks five languages and has served as ambassador from Guinea to other countries
- Received her GED certificate just before her 80th birthday

World History

Unit 3: World History

The world around us is ever-changing. Today, technology, such as the Internet and wireless communication devices, has brought us closer together than ever before. As we look toward the future, countries must collaborate more than ever to ensure success. Before moving forward with our future, however, we must first understand our past.

The importance of world history also extends to the GED Social Studies Test, where it comprises 15 percent of all questions. As with other areas of the GED Tests, world history questions will test your ability to interpret information by using reading skills and thinking skills such as comprehension, application, analysis, and evaluation. In Unit 3, the introduction of more complex reading skills, along with visuals, such as diagrams and timelines, will help you prepare for the GED Social Studies Test.

Table of Contents

Categorize Concepts

① Learn the Skill

When learning about a social studies topic, you will find that information relates to that subject in many different ways. For instance, when learning about a country, you may read about its people, geography, government, economy, and history. By **categorizing concepts** under headings such as these, you can better organize and understand what you have learned.

② Practice the Skill

By mastering the skill of categorizing concepts, you will improve your study and test-taking skills, especially as they relate to the GED Social Studies Test. Read the information and strategies below. Then answer the question that follows.

Ⓐ As you read, look for related topics or ideas in the text. Consider how you might group these ideas together or how you might draw distinctions between them.

Ⓑ Consider how the information relates to subjects with which you are familiar. Do the ideas in this passage fit into a familiar category, such as history or government?

> Some city-states in ancient Greece featured a system of government known as an oligarchy. In an oligarchy, only a select few citizens share ruling power. Sparta became the best-known oligarchic city-state. While its government **Ⓐ** featured kings and an assembly of free men over 30, Sparta's government was actually controlled by a Council of Elders. This group included 28 members and five elected officials. They proposed laws to the assembly, but the assembly lacked the power to debate these proposals.
>
> In the city-state of Athens, citizens established a **Ⓐ** different type of government known as democracy. In Athens, every freeborn man older than 18 received an equal vote in government elections. Many government officials took office through a lottery system and served under term limits. In fact, elections only took place in order to select some of the most important government officials.

☑ TEST-TAKING TIPS

When preparing to categorize concepts, try to identify the main ideas and key details of a passage. Recognizing these items will often point you toward potential categories, such as government or geography, into which information can be placed.

1. In what way could a community in which all adults received an equal vote in choosing local government officials be categorized?

   (1) as an oligarchy
   (2) as a democracy
   (3) as both an oligarchy and a democracy
   (4) as neither an oligarchy nor a democracy
   (5) as a city-state

Directions: Choose the <u>one best answer</u> to each question.

<u>Questions 2 and 3</u> refer to the following information.

While Ancient Egypt was in the desert, the Nile River and its tributaries allowed the Egyptians to have an agrarian society. Wheat and barley were grown in such abundance that the Egyptians could keep vast stores and trade part of their harvest. Domesticated animals, such as cattle, sheep, goats, and pigs, were raised for food, and dogs and cats were kept as pets.

Egyptian families typically consisted of parents and children in one household. Egyptian couples were monogamous, but there were no formal or legal requirements for marriage. Divorce was also possible. Women had almost the same legal rights as men. They could own property and do with it as they saw fit. Women could also begin divorce proceedings. Although they rarely held government office, many women had power as priestesses in Egypt's many religious sects.

2. Which concepts are most important in the text above?

   (1) marriage, domestic pets
   (2) family, geographic
   (3) military, agrarian
   (4) government, religious
   (5) agriculture, daily life

3. How were women in Ancient Egypt best categorized?

   Women in Ancient Egypt

   (1) were farmers
   (2) were artistic
   (3) had many rights
   (4) had nuclear families
   (5) kept cats as pets

<u>Questions 4 and 5</u> refer to the following information and map.

The Greek city-states of Athens and Sparta once cooperated to defend the Greek states from Persian invaders. The Greeks engaged in three major conflicts against these invaders, the last of which took place in 479 BC. Disagreements developed between the two city-states regarding both land and sea trade routes and monies contributed to the rivals by smaller political states. Beginning in 431 BC, the Peloponnesian War lasted for 28 years, with alternating periods of conflict and peace. While both sides had important victories, Sparta ultimately emerged victorious in 404 BC.

4. Examine the map closely. How was Athens best categorized logically?

   (1) as an imperial state
   (2) as a naval power
   (3) as controlled by a pacifist government
   (4) as electing isolationist leaders
   (5) as a nation with many overland trade routes

5. Into which of the following categories would you place the Peloponnesian War?

   (1) skirmish
   (2) cold war
   (3) world war
   (4) civil war
   (5) unresolved conflict

Interpret Diagrams

① Learn the Skill

Diagrams are different from other types of graphics, such as charts or graphs, because they can show the relationships that exist between pieces of information. For instance, diagrams can show sequence, similarities, differences, and other comparisons. Authors often use diagrams to concisely present or summarize social studies information. By learning how to **interpret** diagrams, you can maximize your understanding of the information presented in these visuals.

② Practice the Skill

By mastering the skill of interpreting diagrams, you will improve your study and test-taking skills, especially as they relate to the GED Social Studies Test. Examine the diagram and strategies below. Then answer the question that follows.

A The format of a diagram provides clues to its purpose and the type of information that it will include. A Venn diagram shows how two subjects are similar and different.

B Pay close attention to the titles and headings of diagrams. What information can you learn from these items? Here, the headings above the two main circles identify the subjects that will be compared and contrasted.

12TH AND 13TH CENTURY MONARCHIES

A

England B

Both B

France B

- Instituted new justice system that established common law in England
- *Magna Carta* forced king to grant more authority to barons in 1215
- Parliament established in 1264

- Centralized government
- Made rule over vassals more official
- Increased wealth from new tax systems

- In prior years, king only took authority of area near Paris
- Under Philip II, claimed lands from England
- Philip II established capable administration to facilitate tax collection

---

☑ TEST-TAKING TIPS

When asked to use a diagram in a testing situation, first preview the questions related to the diagram. Determine what information you will need to locate in the diagram to correctly answer these questions.

1. In which of the following ways did France strengthen its monarchy that England did not?

   (1) France centralized its national government.
   (2) France established a new system of justice.
   (3) France granted shared authority to its political bodies.
   (4) France increased wealth from a new tax system.
   (5) France claimed new territories for the nation.

Directions: Choose the <u>one best answer</u> to each question. <u>Questions 2 and 3</u> refer to the following diagram.

ARCHITECTURE IN THE MIDDLE AGES

Churches provided the best examples of these forms of medieval architecture

Romanesque
- End of 11th century
- Common in Benedictine monasteries
- Characterized by round arches in doors, windows, and vaults
- Large structures with heavy stone walls
- Thick columns extending from floor to vault

Gothic
- 12th and 13th century
- Taller buildings; less sprawling than Romanesque churches
- Pointed arches instead of round; designed to make buildings appear more soaring
- Weight supported by flying buttresses

2. Which of the following statements is true?

   (1) Romanesque architecture became popular after Gothic architecture.
   (2) Gothic structures were generally shorter than Romanesque buildings.
   (3) Benedictine monasteries typically used Gothic architecture.
   (4) Romanesque structures did not typically feature flying buttresses.
   (5) Romanesque buildings covered a smaller area than Gothic structures.

3. Why would Gothic churches be more visually dramatic than Romanesque churches?

   Gothic churches

   (1) were built in the 12th and 13th centuries
   (2) had heavy stone walls
   (3) used flying buttresses to support round arches and vaults
   (4) were taller and appeared to be soaring
   (5) had pointed arches and were common in Benedictine monasteries

Questions 4 and 5 refer to the following diagram.

LIFE IN MEDIEVAL COURTS

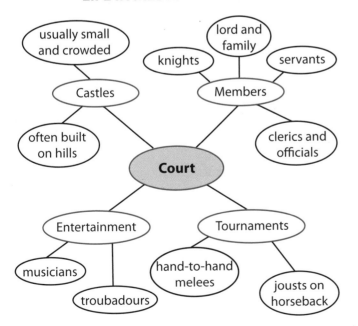

4. The tournaments held at medieval courts are most similar to which present-day event?

   Tournaments were similar to present-day

   (1) concerts
   (2) vacations
   (3) sporting events
   (4) town meetings
   (5) political rallies

5. According to the diagram, how are knights best classified?

   (1) as entertainment for the Court
   (2) as living in castles
   (3) as participating in tournaments
   (4) as having hand-to-hand melees
   (5) as members of the Court

Determine Point of View

① Learn the Skill

Authors write different types of material from a variety of **perspectives** and for a number of different purposes. For instance, a textbook author writes to inform or educate students. On the other hand, a newspaper editorial is written to persuade the reader. The perspective from which a work is written is called the **point of view**.

② Practice the Skill

By mastering the skill of understanding point of view, you will improve your study and test-taking skills, especially as they relate to the GED Social Studies Test. Read the excerpt and strategies below. Then answer the question that follows.

Ⓐ As you read a passage, think about the author's purpose for writing, and how that purpose relates to his or her point of view.

Ⓑ To help determine an author's point of view, look for statements or passages that express opinions about the subjects being discussed. When considered collectively, these opinions will help you identify the author's point of view.

> From the *Magna Carta* (1297):
>
> … Know that we, at the prompting of God and for the health of our soul and the souls of our ancestors and successors, for the glory of holy Church and the improvement of our realm, freely and out of our good will have given and granted to the archbishops, bishops, abbots, priors, earls, barons and all of our realm these liberties written below to hold in our realm of England in perpetuity.
>
> … No freeman is to be taken or imprisoned or disseised of his free tenement or of his liberties or free customs, or outlawed or exiled or in any way ruined, nor will we go against such a man or send against him save by lawful judgement of his peers or by the law of the land.

☑ TEST-TAKING TIPS

When answering test questions related to an author's point of view, first identify the subject or main idea of the writing. Then think about the different perspectives that someone could likely have regarding this topic. This step will allow you to narrow your focus and clarify the author's point of view more quickly.

1. Based on the authors' point of view, what is the purpose of the *Magna Carta*?

   The *Magna Carta* was written to

   (1) improve the Church
   (2) establish basic rights of Englishmen
   (3) grant more power to archbishops
   (4) overthrow the monarchy
   (5) establish church courts to ensure liberties

Directions: Choose the one best answer to each question.

Questions 2 through 4 refer to the following excerpt.

From John Locke's *Two Treatises of Government* (1690):

Sect. 4. To understand political power right, and derive it from its original, we must consider, what state all men are naturally in, and that is, a state of perfect freedom to order their actions, and dispose of their possessions and persons, as they think fit, within the bounds of the law of nature, without asking leave, or depending upon the will of any other man.

A state also of equality, wherein all the power and jurisdiction is reciprocal, no one having more than another; there being nothing more evident, than that creatures of the same species and rank, promiscuously born to all the same advantages of nature, and the use of the same faculties, should also be equal one amongst another without subordination or subjection, unless the lord and master of them all [God] should, by any manifest declaration of his will, set one above another, and confer on him, by an evident and clear appointment, an undoubted right to dominion and sovereignty.

2. In this passage, what is Locke's point of view about people?

   Locke argues that people are naturally

   (1) evil
   (2) selfish
   (3) free
   (4) trustworthy
   (5) unequal

3. What is Locke's point of view about government in this excerpt?

   (1) There should be no government because all men are free and natural.
   (2) Government should consist of people born into a certain rank.
   (3) Government should limit how people can dispose of their possessions.
   (4) Those in government should establish jurisdiction and subjection.
   (5) Government should promote equality and only be led by a divinely-appointed sovereign.

4. How does Locke's point of view compare with Thomas Jefferson's?

   (1) They both supported the monarchy.
   (2) They both believed that some men were born to rule others.
   (3) They both believed that man has natural rights.
   (4) They both supported a powerful national government.
   (5) They both disagreed with the idea of equality.

Question 5 refers to the following quotation.

"The marble not yet carved can hold the form Of every thought the greatest artist has."

From Michelangelo Buonarroti, *Sonnet 15*

5. Which of the following correctly states Michelangelo's point of view in the quotation above?

   Michelangelo believed that

   (1) each new sculpture offered an opportunity for greatness
   (2) sculpture was the most important form of fine art
   (3) many sculptors did not recognize the quality of their work
   (4) too many sculptors relied on the great ideas of other artists
   (5) marble was the most challenging medium in which to perfect a sculpture

Draw Conclusions

1 Learn the Skill

You have already learned that an inference is an educated guess based on facts or evidence. By combining several inferences to make a judgment, you can **draw conclusions**. The ability to draw conclusions enables you to develop new ideas about social studies material. In this way, you can gain a deeper understanding of the information you read.

2 Practice the Skill

By mastering the skill of drawing conclusions, you will improve your study and test-taking skills, especially as they relate to the GED Social Studies Test. Read the information and strategies below. Then answer the question that follows.

A As you read, look for pieces of information about which you can ask questions, such as: Why would Britain want a survey of India? What pieces of information might you need to answer such a question?

B Remember that an inference is like a puzzle that must be put together using two or more pieces of information. These educated guesses can then be combined to form a larger conclusion. You can also call upon your own prior knowledge to help you draw conclusions.

One of the most important geographical projects of the 1800s was the Great Trigonometrical Survey of India. **A** Britain had expanded its commercial and colonial interests in India during the 1700s, and the government wished to learn more about the region. As a result, the government launched the Great Trigonometrical Survey of India in 1800. The goal of this project was to survey and map the Indian subcontinent, along with those areas extending north of the Himalayas. **B** Because Nepal and Tibet forbid the British surveyors from entering their borders, the British asked Indians to disguise themselves as Buddhist pilgrims and secretly survey these areas. These volunteers learned how to measure a mile by taking 2,000 steps. In all, the Great Trigonometrical Survey of India took 70 years to complete.

USING LOGIC

In order to answer this question, you will have to use logic and call upon your prior knowledge. Think about why a country would not want representatives of another country on its land.

1. Why do you think the British surveyors were forbidden to travel in Nepal and Tibet?

(1) The nations were worried about British colonial ambitions.
(2) The mountainous terrain was very dangerous.
(3) The governments of these nations did not want maps made of their territories.
(4) Leaders from these nations feared the spread of Buddhism to Britain.
(5) Britain had become a strong ally of India.

Directions: Choose the one best answer to each question.

Questions 2 and 3 refer to the following information.

European exploration of Australia focused on the charting of the continent's coastal areas, as well as the exploration of its interior. Between 1798 and 1803, Matthew Flinders, a British navigator, sailed around the continent. Though Flinders had expected to locate numerous large river mouths during this charting expedition, he identified far fewer of these places along the coast than he had anticipated. This stirred discussion that the rivers on the west side of the Great Dividing Range could empty into a sizable inland body of water. Explorers later determined that these rivers instead joined the Murray River and emptied into the Indian Ocean.

Early explorers who attempted to cross the continent often encountered great difficulty. Some individuals even lost their lives. Despite many conflicts with Aboriginal Australians along the way, Scottish explorer John McDouall Stuart successfully crossed the continent from south to north in 1862. Later, Aboriginal Australians served as guides for other European explorers. These explorers helped to eventually map the entire Australian continent.

2. Why were the British so anxious to explore Australian rivers?

   (1) They wanted to find the Great Dividing Range.
   (2) They wanted to create a map of the continent.
   (3) They were searching for an easy way to explore the continent's interior.
   (4) They were anxious to find gold or diamonds on the continent.
   (5) They quickly wanted to control the continent.

3. Why did European explorers likely experience conflicts with Aboriginal Australians?

   Conflict likely occurred because of

   (1) political allegiances
   (2) the Aborigines' fear of British imperial ambitions
   (3) disagreements about routes across the continent
   (4) arguments over naming rights of landmarks on new maps of the continent
   (5) efforts to control the continent's large inland body of water

Question 4 refers to the following table.

THE RACE TO THE SOUTH POLE		
EXPEDITION LEADER	**DATE**	**OUTCOME**
Robert Falcon Scott	1901–1904	Ventured closer to South Pole than any previous expeditions
Ernest Shackleton	1907–1909	Approached within 200 km of the South Pole
Roald Amundsen	1911	Led the first expedition to reach South Pole in December of 1911
Robert Falcon Scott	1911–1912	Arrived at South Pole five weeks after Amundsen expedition; Scott and crew died on return journey

4. Which of the following most likely posed the greatest obstacle to reaching the South Pole?

   (1) a lack of supplies
   (2) dangerous animals
   (3) native inhabitants
   (4) poorly-built ships
   (5) cold temperatures

Interpret Timelines

① Learn the Skill

The ability to **interpret timelines** proves especially valuable when studying history. Timelines present sequences of events in a visual manner. This enables us to determine not only the order in which the events occurred, but also the intervals that fell between these events. Because timelines show key events in sequence, it is possible to identify historical trends that connect those events.

② Practice the Skill

By mastering the skill of interpreting timelines, you will improve your study and test-taking skills, especially as they relate to the GED Social Studies Test. Read the timeline below. Then answer the question that follows.

Ⓐ The benchmark dates on a timeline show the equivalent intervals into which the full time span of the timeline is divided. In this case, the timeline shows the period from 1915 to 1935 divided into five-year intervals.

Ⓑ This timeline illustrates the events that led to Hitler becoming chancellor of Germany. The trend here connects Germany's humiliation after World War I to Hitler building the Nazi Party into a national party to economic depression and political dissatisfaction and to the rise of Hitler and the Nazi Party.

POST-WORLD WAR I AND HITLER'S RISE TO POWER

1915—

1918: World War I ends

1919: Ⓑ Treaty of Versailles imposes harsh penalties on Germany for its role in the war

1920—

1921: Hitler becomes leader of the Nazi Party in Germany

1923: Hitler leads a failed attempt to overthrow the Bavarian government

1925—

1925–1930: Ⓑ Hitler works to build the Nazi Party throughout Germany

1929: Ⓑ Depression reaches Germany, leading to dissatisfaction with other political parties

1930—

1932: Ⓑ Nazi candidates receive most votes of any party in German elections

1935—

1933: Hitler becomes chancellor of Germany

USING LOGIC

Timelines typically show a trend in events. Events on the timeline are usually connected. By reviewing each event and what occurred before and after, you should be able to see a trend.

1. What directly led to the Nazi Party receiving the most votes in the 1932 German elections?

   (1) the end of World War I in 1918
   (2) the choice of Hitler to lead the Nazi Party
   (3) victorious allies act punitively towards the Germans at Versailles
   (4) the Germans were unhappy with other politicians because of the economic crisis
   (5) the attempted overthrow of the Bavarian government

UNIT 3

Directions: Choose the one best answer to each question.

Questions 2 and 3 refer to the following timeline.

GERMAN INVASIONS

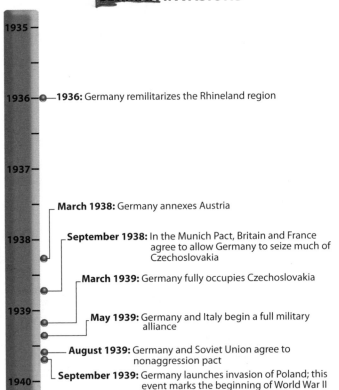

Questions 4 and 5 refer to the following timeline.

ATTACKS ON BRITAIN AND FRANCE

2. Which of the following trends is supported by the information in the timeline?

   (1) Germany's main desire was to conquer Britain.
   (2) Germany's actions were hesitant and weak.
   (3) Germany showed its strength, and many European countries gave in.
   (4) Germany was opposed at every turn by a united Europe.
   (5) Germany and the Soviet Union would be allies in the upcoming war.

3. Which prior event **MOST** affected the actions shown on the timeline?

   (1) the unification of German states
   (2) Hitler's election as chancellor
   (3) the Great Depression
   (4) the Franco-Prussian War
   (5) World War I

4. The information on the timeline supports which of the following conclusions?

   (1) Hitler focused his attacks on London.
   (2) World War II would be over quickly.
   (3) Germany won the Battle of Britain.
   (4) The British refused to surrender to Germany.
   (5) It took a year for Germany to secure France.

5. The timeline supports which of the following statements?

   (1) Hitler was confident of victory in the summer of 1940.
   (2) The German air force was invincible.
   (3) Gaining France was not strategically beneficial to Germany.
   (4) Italy and France were allies.
   (5) French premier Pétain gave Hitler his first victory.

Generalize

① Learn the Skill

When you **generalize,** you make a broad statement that applies to entire groups of people, places, events, and so on. These statements typically contain words such as *usually, all, everyone, many, few, often,* or *overall*. Generalizing is useful to draw a basic conclusion about something, for example, *The United States is a multi-cultural country*. However, beware of false conclusions and inaccurate generalizations. Be sure to examine all the information before making a generalization.

② Practice the Skill

By mastering the skill of generalizing, you will improve your study and test-taking skills, especially as they relate to the GED Social Studies Test. Read the information and strategies below and then answer the question that follows.

A Look for words, such as *generally, most,* or *many,* as well as those listed above, that typically signal a generalization is being made. Then, look closely at the statement that follows to determine whether the writer applies it to a large group of items.

B When you identify a generalization in a passage of text, look closely to see what facts or evidence the author includes to support his or her statement.

💡 USING LOGIC

As you encounter generalizations, you can classify them as either valid or invalid. A valid generalization is supported by facts and examples. On the other hand, an invalid generalization cannot be supported using facts and examples.

The communist government of East Germany constructed the Berlin Wall in 1961 to prevent East Germans from fleeing the communist nation for the democratic nation of West Germany. East German troops heavily guarded the wall to prevent crossings. While a few citizens managed to cross this boundary, <u>most</u> people attempting to cross into West Berlin lost their lives. Those on the East German side of the wall <u>generally</u> had a lower standard of living compared to their Western counterparts, <u>similar to the way people in the Soviet Union lived versus people in France</u>. However, by the summer of 1989, the Hungarian government began to allow East Germans to travel through Hungary in order to reach Austria and West Germany. This development rendered the wall obsolete. By the fall of 1989, the East German government had nearly collapsed. On November 9, the government granted citizens the freedom to move across the boundary into West Germany. East Germany and West Germany reunited as a single nation the following year.

1. Which of the following generalizations does the author make in this passage?

   East Germans generally

   (1) did not cross successfully from East Germany to West Berlin
   (2) directed their attempts to escape toward Hungary
   (3) enjoyed the freedom to travel as they wished
   (4) viewed West Germany as a hostile nation
   (5) wished to remain in East Germany

Directions: Choose the one best answer to each question.

Questions 2 and 3 refer to the following excerpt.

Summary of the Dayton Peace Agreement on Bosnia-Herzegovina, released by the U.S. Department of State, November 30, 1995:

General Framework Agreement

- Bosnia and Herzegovina, Croatia and the Federal Republic of Yugoslavia [FRY] agree to fully respect the sovereign equality of one another and to settle disputes by peaceful means.

- The FRY and Bosnia and Herzegovina recognize each other, and agree to discuss further aspects of their mutual recognition.

- The parties agree to fully respect and promote fulfillment of the commitments made in the various Annexes, and they obligate themselves to respect human rights and the rights of refugees and displaced persons.

- The parties agree to cooperate fully with all entities, including those authorized by the United Nations Security Council, in implementing the peace settlement and investigating and prosecuting war crimes and other violations of international humanitarian law.

2. Which of the following generalizations is supported by the excerpt?

   (1) The nations that signed this agreement are committed to preserving peace in the future.
   (2) Bosnia and Yugoslavia will join together as one nation.
   (3) The agreement was released by the U.S. Department of State on November 30, 1995.
   (4) The parties will probably establish courts to prosecute war crimes and blame one another for all atrocities.
   (5) The nations generally disagreed with the motives of the U.S. State Department.

3. Which of the following generalizations can be made about the nations involved in this agreement?

   These nations were all generally

   (1) non-democratic governments
   (2) located in Eastern Europe
   (3) against this agreement
   (4) suspicious of the authority of the United Nations
   (5) guilty of war crimes

Questions 4 and 5 refer to the following information.

The official currency of the European Union (EU), the euro, went into circulation for 12 of the 27 member states on January 1, 2002. These nations were Spain, Portugal, the Netherlands, Luxembourg, Italy, Ireland, Greece, Germany, France, Finland, Belgium, and Austria. Since then, Slovenia, Cyprus, and Malta have also adopted the euro. The euro was designed as part of a plan to unify the members of the EU around a single form of currency. Members of the EU had to meet a strict set of qualifications before adopting the euro, in order to give the euro an acceptable level of stability.

4. All members of the European Union adopted the euro as their unit of currency.

   Which of the following nations could be cited to show that this generalization is invalid?

   (1) Portugal
   (2) Spain
   (3) Ireland
   (4) the United Kingdom
   (5) the United States

5. The information supports which of the following generalizations?

   (1) Countries generally joined the European Union for economic reasons.
   (2) Most of the countries in the European Union are in Eastern Europe.
   (3) Countries often join the European Union.
   (4) Overall, the currencies of European countries are unstable.
   (5) New denominations of the euro are usually designed by different member countries.

Unit 3 Review

The Unit Review is structured to resemble the GED Social Studies Test. Be sure to read each question and all possible answers very carefully before choosing your answer.

To record your answers, fill in the numbered circle that corresponds to the answer you select for each question in the Unit Review.

Do not rest your pencil on the answer area while considering your answer. Make no stray or unnecessary marks. If you change an answer, erase your first mark completely.

Mark only one answer space for each question; multiple answers will be scored as incorrect.

Sample Question

What was the main cause for the Third Crusade?

(1) Pope Urban II wanted to control the Holy Land.
(2) Muslim leader Saladin had recaptured Jerusalem.
(3) English King Richard the Lionheart wanted to capture Constantinople.
(4) The Muslims had reclaimed Edessa.
(5) Pope Eugenius II threatened those who would not join the crusade.

①●③④⑤

Questions 1 and 2 refer to the following timeline.

THE UNITED NATIONS

late 1939: First concrete plan for a new international organization was started within the U.S. State Department

January 1942: First official use of the name United Nations

October 1943: Moscow Declaration expresses need for a new organization to replace the League of Nations

August–October 1944: China, Britain, the Soviet Union, and the United States write proposals for new organization's charter

February 1945: Nations reach additional agreements on these measures

April–June 1945: Founding conference for United Nations is held in San Francisco

October 1945: United Nations charter is ratified

January 1946: First meeting of General Assembly in London

December 1946: General Assembly receives $8.5 million from John D. Rockefeller, Jr., to buy land in New York City for its headquarters

1. What was taking place when China, Britain, the Soviet Union, and the United States were writing proposals for the U.N. charter?

(1) the Great Depression
(2) World War I
(3) World War II
(4) the Korean War
(5) the Cold War

①②③④⑤

2. Based on the timeline, why was this group of nations so eager to establish the United Nations by the end of 1945?

The nations wanted

(1) to form a new group to take over when the League of Nations' charter ran out
(2) to organize humanitarian aid for East Germany
(3) to establish their organization before President Harry Truman left office
(4) to band together in time to punish Japan
(5) to help rebuild Europe and forestall another war

①②③④⑤

Although European explorers reached Australia during the 1600s, very few Europeans took an interest in the continent until British explorer James Cook studied the fertile land of its east coast in 1770. Cook claimed this area for Britain and paved the way for Australia's first European settlement. Built in 1788, this settlement served as a British penal colony. For many years, Britain continued to send individuals to Australia that had declared bankruptcy or been convicted of crimes. The entire Australian continent became a dependency of Britain in 1829. Exploration of Australia continued throughout much of the 1800s. Sheep and wheat became important agricultural products in the early part of the century. Beginning in 1851, a series of gold strikes made mining another important component of the Australian economy. The continent's growing economy also brought permanent settlements, which replaced the penal colonies by the middle of the 1800s.

3. What conclusion can you draw about Europeans' interest in Australia following James Cook's exploration of the continent's east coast?

   (1) They hoped to find gold.
   (2) They hoped to raise cattle.
   (3) They hoped to build permanent settlements.
   (4) They hoped to establish a port for shipping.
   (5) They hoped to farm the fertile soil.
   ① ② ③ ④ ⑤

4. Why might the British have wanted to send debtors and people convicted of crimes to Australia?

   (1) They were experienced farmers.
   (2) It relieved the strain on the penal system in Britain.
   (3) It would prevent non-criminal British from moving to Australia.
   (4) It would allow the British to establish colonies in Asia.
   (5) They could explore the continent and send reports back to Britain.
   ① ② ③ ④ ⑤

The arts were one of the many areas of life that changed significantly during the Renaissance. A spirit of innovation in society led artists working in mediums such as architecture, sculpture, and painting, to introduce new techniques that differed from medieval methods. Renaissance communities provided supportive environments for artists as well. As towns gained wealth during this period, money was often set aside to support local artists. Whereas paintings and sculptures had previously been created primarily for use in churches, affluent citizens and royal court members gradually became important patrons of the arts. The arts also reflected the Renaissance's combining of the arts and science, as artists began to use principles of mathematics and geometry in order to create a sense of perspective and proportion in their work.

5. What generalization can you make about the arts during the Renaissance?

   During the Renaissance, the arts generally

   (1) found little support in local communities
   (2) received patronage only from churches
   (3) became more respected and supported
   (4) generated less enthusiasm than developments in mathematics and geometry
   (5) received attention only when merged with the study of science
   ① ② ③ ④ ⑤

6. How does the author of this passage view the Renaissance?

   The author views the Renaissance as a period of

   (1) innovation
   (2) conflict
   (3) prosperity
   (4) despair
   (5) reflection
   ① ② ③ ④ ⑤

Questions 7 and 8 refer to the following information.

In the early 1700s, India's once-powerful Mughal Empire had begun to decline, while British power expanded. The trading company known as the English East India Company arrived during the 1600s and constructed a fort at Calcutta. From this location, the company eventually conquered the Indian subcontinent. British officers commanded an army of Indians that helped to take over the region. This army remained a powerful force in Asia until India gained its independence in 1947.

7. What conclusion can you draw based on the information in this paragraph?

   (1) The English East India Company struggled to make a profit in India.
   (2) Calcutta was a small city.
   (3) India gained its independence from Britain.
   (4) The Mughal Empire declined due to a lack of trade.
   (5) British officers in India had little experience leading troops.

   ① ② ③ ④ ⑤

8. Under which of the following subjects would you categorize the main ideas of this paragraph?

   The main ideas are best categorized as

   (1) geography
   (2) social history
   (3) ancient Indus Valley culture
   (4) colonialism
   (5) citizenship and government

   ① ② ③ ④ ⑤

Questions 9 and 10 refer to the following diagram.

THE INCA

| The Inca gradually extended their authority over other groups living in the Andes region between 1200 and 1440. |

↓

| After 1493, the empire later began a period of civil war. This conflict ended as Spanish explorers began to arrive. |

↓

| Spanish explorer Francisco Pizarro reached South America in 1532. He executed Inca emperor Atahualpa and began conquest of the Inca Empire. |

↓

| Pizarro's forces entered the central Inca city of Cuzco in 1533. The Inca eventually fell under Spanish rule and received subordinate status. |

9. Based on the information in the diagram above, which of the following statements is correct?

   (1) The Inca had significant interaction with European explorers prior to Pizarro's arrival in 1532.
   (2) The period in which the Inca extended their influence lasted more than 200 years.
   (3) The civil war within the Inca civilization broke out after 1533.
   (4) The Inca did not resist Spanish conquest of their region.
   (5) The Inca remained dominant even after Spanish conquest.

   ① ② ③ ④ ⑤

10. Inca leader Huayna Capac conquered the kingdom of Quito, or present-day Ecuador. This marked the height of Incan expansion and authority.

   Where should the above information be added to the diagram?

   (1) before the first box
   (2) between the first and second boxes
   (3) inside the second box
   (4) inside the third box
   (5) after the fourth box

   ① ② ③ ④ ⑤

Questions 11 and 12 refer to the following information.

The culture of ancient Greece valued diversity, and Greek mythology came to reflect this. The ancient Greeks worshipped many different deities and did not adhere to a strict set of beliefs. Instead, they told a wide variety of stories about Greek gods. These tales often differed according to whether they were told in the form of epic poetry, comedies, or tragedies.

In ancient Rome, the people originally viewed gods as a series of powers, rather than as individuals. The interaction of ancient Greek and Roman cultures during the 6th century BC influenced the Romans to describe gods in human form. During the final three centuries BC, Roman authors began to apply the names of Roman gods to Greek traditions. This practice created what is known as Greco-Roman mythology.

11. How might you best describe Greek mythology?

Greek mythology could best be described as

(1) strict
(2) unchanging
(3) unified
(4) varied
(5) prehistoric

①②③④⑤

12. Under which of the following headings could you categorize Roman mythology?

(1) common modern-day religions
(2) highly organized religions
(3) intolerant systems of belief
(4) influenced Greek mythology
(5) influenced by Greek mythology

①②③④⑤

Questions 13 and 14 refer to the following table.

EUROPEAN ECONOMIC COMMUNITY/ EUROPEAN UNION MEMBERSHIP	
YEAR JOINED	NATION
1958	Belgium, West Germany, France, Italy, Luxembourg, the Netherlands
1973	Denmark, Ireland, the United Kingdom
1981	Greece
1986	Spain, Portugal
1990	territory from former East Germany
1995	Austria, Finland, Sweden
2004	Czech Republic, Estonia, Cyprus, Latvia, Lithuania, Hungary, Malta, Poland, Slovenia, Slovakia
2007	Bulgaria, Romania

13. Why did the majority of Eastern European countries not join the European Economic Community/European Union until 2004?

They did not join until 2004 because

(1) they were barred by France and Germany
(2) they did not accept the euro as their currency until that time
(3) they were prevented by the former East Germany
(4) they had been part of the Soviet Union
(5) up until that time, the EU only allowed two countries to join per year

①②③④⑤

14. Based on the information in the table, which of the following statements is correct?

(1) Ireland joined the organization more than 20 years before Hungary.
(2) Belgium joined the organization in 1973.
(3) Austria joined the organization in the same year as Hungary.
(4) The United Kingdom was one of the original members of the organization.
(5) Spain joined the organization earlier than France.

①②③④⑤

Questions 15 and 16 refer to the following excerpt from Thomas Hobbes's *Leviathan*.

And because the condition of man … is a condition of war of every one against everyone, in which case every one is governed by his own reason, and there is nothing he can make use of that may not be a help unto him in preserving his life against his enemies; it followeth that in such a condition every man has a right to every thing, even to one another's body. And therefore, as long as this natural right of every man to every thing endureth, there can be no security to any man, how strong or wise soever he be, of living out the time which nature ordinarily alloweth men to live. And consequently it is a precept, or general rule of reason: that every man ought to endeavour peace, as far as he has hope of obtaining it; and when he cannot obtain it, that he may seek and use all helps and advantages of war. The first branch of which rule containeth the first and fundamental law of nature, which is: to seek peace and follow it. The second, the sum of the right of nature, which is: by all means we can defend ourselves.

15. What is Hobbes's point of view?

  (1) People should use whatever means necessary to defend themselves.
  (2) People should not seek to live together in peace.
  (3) No person has the right to take another's property.
  (4) Man is inherently unselfish.
  (5) Governments should not use the power of war, even when necessary.

  ① ② ③ ④ ⑤

16. Which of the following would use Hobbes's writings to support their own point of view?

  (1) a person seeking to unite warring groups
  (2) a monarch offering protection in exchange for reduced individual rights
  (3) a political leader who does not support the use of force to defend a territory
  (4) a religious leader arguing that religious bodies should hold more power than political bodies
  (5) a philosopher arguing that man is inherently good

  ① ② ③ ④ ⑤

Questions 17 and 18 refer to the following information.

The Shang Dynasty ruled ancient China from approximately 1570 BC to 1045 BC. Archaeological evidence suggests that the Shang Dynasty featured a complex society. This society included agricultural workers, as well as urban artisans and priests. Because the earliest written records of ancient China date to this period, scholars consider the Shang to be China's first historical dynasty. Most of these Shang Dynasty writings are carvings or inscriptions on animal bones or shells. Shang Dynasty kings used these items to make predictions about the future, and the writings on these bones and shells record the kings' predictions. A king might issue predictions on topics as varied as military strategy, weather, harvests, family, and the construction of settlements. In this way, these inscriptions provide a valuable account of the daily lives of Shang Dynasty kings.

17. Why was the Shang Dynasty considered to be China's first historical dynasty?

  (1) because it featured a complex society
  (2) because both agricultural workers and urban artisans worked in the society
  (3) because Shang rulers controlled China from approximately 1570 BC to 1045 BC.
  (4) because the earliest written records of ancient China date to this period
  (5) because Shang kings used animal bones and shells to make predictions

  ① ② ③ ④ ⑤

18. How are the Shang Dynasty writings and carvings best categorized?

  (1) religious
  (2) political
  (3) militaristic
  (4) agricultural
  (5) geographical

  ① ② ③ ④ ⑤

WORLD WAR I

Causes

- Nationalism in Austria-Hungary
- Rivalry between France and Germany
- European nations' imperialism leads to territorial disputes in Asia and Africa
- Conflicts cause the formation of extensive alliances and an arms race
- Serbian nationalist assassinates Archduke Ferdinand of Austria-Hungary
- Following Ferdinand's assassination, alliances draw many nations into the conflict, making it a world war
- Britain was determined to keep its colonial territories and feared that unless they entered the war, Germany would control Western Europe.

Outcomes

- Treaty of Versailles forces Germany to accept responsibility for war; ordered to pay costly reparations
- War brings end to Austro-Hungarian, Russian, and German empires
- League of Nations forms in an effort to promote cooperation to prevent future wars
- More than 10 million soldiers lose their lives
- Women enter many historically male occupations
- Many nations fall into economic hardships due to the expense of war

UNIT 3

19. Which of the following was most responsible for turning the conflicts that started World War I into a world war?

    (1) nationalism in Austria-Hungary
    (2) territorial disputes in Asia
    (3) European imperialism in Africa
    (4) an arms race among European nations
    (5) extensive alliances formed among nations
    ① ② ③ ④ ⑤

20. In which historically male occupation did women likely work during the war?

    During World War I, women most likely worked as

    (1) political office holders
    (2) coal miners
    (3) physicians
    (4) industrial workers
    (5) soldiers
    ① ② ③ ④ ⑤

21. The rivalry between which two nations became an important cause of World War I?

    (1) Austria and Hungary
    (2) Serbia and Germany
    (3) Britain and Germany
    (4) Russia and Austria-Hungary
    (5) the United States and France
    ① ② ③ ④ ⑤

22. Which event did the post-World War I appeasement of Germany lead to?

    This policy eventually led to

    (1) the Great Depression
    (2) the election of Franklin D. Roosevelt
    (3) a stock market crash
    (4) World War II
    (5) the formation of the League of Nations
    ① ② ③ ④ ⑤

RUTH ANN MINNER

Ruth Ann Minner was never one to back away from a challenge. Minner, raised on a small farm in Delaware, left high school at age 16 to help support her family. She later married, but the sudden death of her husband led Minner to pursue—and earn—a GED certificate while working two jobs and raising three sons.

In 1974, Minner entered politics, serving in the Delaware House of Representatives until 1982. She then served three terms in the state Senate from 1982–1993, when she became lieutenant governor. Eight years later, in 2001, Minner became Delaware's first female governor.

Education has long been one of Governor Minner's priorities. In 2005, she created the Student Excellence Equal Degree (SEED) Scholarship program which enables students in good standing to earn associate's degrees in Delaware for free. As she said,

> **❝ I want to encourage every student in Delaware to work hard, stay focused on school, and know that college is within reach. ❞**

Earning her GED certificate was a challenge Minner (left, with Vice President Joe Biden) was willing to take in order to succeed. Now she helps others achieve success.

Minner has also worked to protect the environment and improve healthcare in Delaware. Thanks in part to her efforts, the rate of cancer in Delaware is four times lower than the national average. Today, Minner lives on a farm in Delaware, just as she did as a child. Her life, however, is much different today than when she left school at age 16. Along with her own life, Minner has improved the lives of many others.

BIO BLAST: Ruth Ann Minner

- Left school at age 16 to work on her family's farm
- Received her GED certificate while raising three sons and working two jobs
- Served four terms in the state House of Representatives and three terms in the state Senate
- Served as Delaware's lieutenant governor for eight years
- Became the first female governor of Delaware in 2001

U.S. Government/Civics

Unit 4: U.S. Government/Civics

The United States uses a democratic form of government. In a democracy, leaders represent the interests of the citizens who elect them. As citizens of the United States, we have various rights and responsibilities. Every time you vote for leaders and issues, you are exercising one of those rights. Similarly, as citizens we also have certain responsibilities. One such responsibility involves staying informed about current events.

The importance of government and civics extends to the GED Social Studies Test, where it makes up 25 percent of all questions. As with other areas of the GED Tests, government and civics questions will test your ability to interpret information by using reading skills and thinking skills such as comprehension, application, analysis, and evaluation. In Unit 4, the introduction of various critical-thinking skills, along with specialized instruction about text and maps, will help you prepare for the GED Social Studies Test.

Table of Contents

Use Context Clues

① Learn the Skill

The **context** of a word or term includes the words, details, and ideas surrounding it. **Context clues** are the pieces of information surrounding an unfamiliar term that help to clarify its meaning. By using context clues, you can determine the meaning of an unfamiliar word or clarify the main points of a confusing passage of text.

② Practice the Skill

By mastering the skill of using context clues, you will improve your study and test-taking skills, especially as they relate to the GED Social Studies Test. Read the excerpt and strategies below. Then answer the question that follows.

Ⓐ The context of this information tells you that it describes the content of a proposition, or a proposed law that voters will either approve or reject. The likely audience for this excerpt includes prospective voters.

Ⓑ Context clues can help you determine the meanings of unfamiliar terms such as *jurisdiction, fast-tracks,* and *rights-of-way.* Nearby terms and phrases, such as "regulatory matters," "approval," and "transmission of renewable energy," can help point you to the correct meaning of each term.

> <u>Prop 7</u>
>
> Renewable Energy Generation. Initiative Statute.
> - Requires utilities, including government-owned utilities, to generate 20% of their power from renewable energy by 2010, a standard currently applicable only to private electrical corporations.
> - Raises requirement for utilities to 40% by 2020 and 50% by 2025.
> - Imposes penalties, subject to waiver, for noncompliance.
> - Transfers some <u>jurisdiction</u> of regulatory matters from Public Utilities Commission to Energy Commission.
> - <u>Fast-tracks</u> approval for new renewable energy plants.
> - Requires utilities to sign longer contracts (20 year minimum) to procure renewable energy.
> - Creates account to purchase <u>rights-of-way</u> and facilities for the transmission of renewable energy.
>
> From Official Voter Information Guide, California General Election, 2008

☑ TEST-TAKING TIPS

When answering a difficult question, you can look for context clues that might suggest one possible answer over another. Further, when reading text passages for a test, use context clues to clarify any information that seems unclear or confusing.

1. What does "jurisdiction" probably mean?

   (1) a group of people
   (2) a list of rules
   (3) the right to make judgments
   (4) the obligation to lead meetings
   (5) a regulatory agency

UNIT 4

Directions: Choose the one best answer to each question.

Question 2 refers to the following information.

From the city charter of Alexandria, Virginia
Section 3.01 Composition of the Council.
The council shall consist of the mayor and six members at large, elected as provided in chapter 10 of this charter, and they shall serve for terms of three years or until their successors shall have been elected and take office ...

2. Which of the following sentences means the same as the details in the charter?

   (1) The council has six members who serve three terms until another member is elected.
   (2) The council has seven members who serve three-year terms until a new mayor is elected.
   (3) The council consists of the mayor and six members from specific districts within the city who each serve three-year terms.
   (4) The council consists of the mayor and six members from any part of the city who serve three-year terms each or until a new member is elected.
   (5) The council consists of the mayor and six members who serve three terms each or until a new council member is elected to take his or her place.

Question 3 refers to the following table.

FEDERAL AND STATE POWERS	
FEDERAL	**STATE**
Has supremacy over conflicting state law	Maintain militia to be called on during local emergencies
Make treaties and declare war	Make marriage and divorce laws
Impose taxes on imports	Organize elections

3. Based on the context of the table, which of the following is most likely a federal power?

   (1) protect public safety
   (2) keep a peacetime army
   (3) organize education
   (4) tax property
   (5) run school boards

Questions 4 and 5 refer to the following information.

CREDIT CARD APPLICATION

Please complete all information below in ink. Missing information may affect our credit decision.

1. PERSONAL INFORMATION

| FIRST NAME | MI | LAST NAME | SOCIAL SECURITY NUMBER | DATE OF BIRTH |
| | | | | MO DAY YR |

| HOME ADDRESS: NUMBER, STREET NAME (APT. #) | HOME PHONE NUMBER ( ) | PERMANENT ☐YES |
| | | US RESIDENT ☐ NO |

CITY   STATE   ZIP   EMAIL ADDRESS

| PLACE OF RESIDENCE | MO RENT/MORTGAGE PAYMENT | HOW LONG AT CURRENT ADDRESS |
| ☐OWN ☐RENT ☐PARENTS ☐OTHER | $ | YRS.   MOS. |

PREVIOUS STREET ADDRESS IF LESS THAN 6 MONTHS AT CURRENT ADDRESS

PREVIOUS CITY   STATE   ZIP

| EMPLOYER/NAME | BUSINESS PHONE ( ) |

| BUSINESS ADDRESS | YOUR POSITION |

CITY   STATE   ZIP

| HOW LONG EMPLOYED | GROSS MONTHLY SALARY | OTHER MONTHLY INCOME* | OTHER INCOME SOURCE* |
| YRS   MOS. | $ | $ | |

*OTHER INCOME: Alimony, child support or separate maintenance income need not be revealed if you do not wish to have it considered as a basis for repaying this obligation.

4. To what is the application referring with the phrase "this obligation?"

   (1) alimony
   (2) child support
   (3) credit card debt
   (4) mortgage
   (5) personal loan

5. Based on the credit card application, what is probably the most important factor for creditors?

   (1) employment history
   (2) citizenship status
   (3) place of residence
   (4) ability to pay debt
   (5) amount of mortgage payment

UNIT 4

Interpret the Constitution

① Learn the Skill

The **United States Constitution**, which outlines the basic principles on which the federal government operates, includes a preamble and seven articles. Twenty-seven amendments have also been added to this document. Because the Constitution describes these principles in a general manner, it becomes important to **interpret** the Constitution in order to understand how its principles apply to the everyday workings of our national government.

② Practice the Skill

By mastering the skill of interpreting the Constitution, you will improve your study and test-taking skills, especially as they relate to the GED Social Studies Test. Read the excerpt and strategies below. Then answer the questions that follow.

A The initial words of the Preamble identify the perspective from which the Constitution is written. With this phrase, the authors of the Constitution indicate that they have written this document on behalf of all Americans.

B These phrases represent examples of the types of general principles discussed in the U.S. Constitution.

From the Preamble to the United States Constitution:

A We the people of the United States, in order to form a more perfect union, establish justice, insure domestic tranquility, provide for the common defense, promote the general welfare, and secure the blessings of liberty to ourselves and our posterity, do ordain and establish this Constitution for the United States of America.

☑ **TEST-TAKING TIPS**

Because the original articles of the U.S. Constitution were written in the late 1700s, the language includes words that may seem confusing or unfamiliar. When interpreting information from the Constitution, look for familiar words and phrases that can provide clues to the meanings of these unfamiliar concepts.

1. Which of the following best describes the meaning of the phrase "insure domestic tranquility"?

   (1) protect the nation from outside threats
   (2) establish a fair and balanced court system
   (3) protect the rights of all people
   (4) maintain peace within the nation
   (5) help all citizens achieve success

2. Which of the following best describes the Preamble?

   (1) an outline
   (2) a declaration
   (3) an apology
   (4) a generalization
   (5) an amendment

UNIT 4

Directions: Choose the one best answer to each question.

Questions 3 and 4 refer to the following excerpt.

From Article I of the U.S. Constitution:

Section 7. All bills for raising revenue shall originate in the House of Representatives; but the Senate may propose or concur with amendments as on other bills.

Every bill which shall have passed the House of Representatives and the Senate, shall, before it become a law, be presented to the President of the United States; if he approve he shall sign it, but if not he shall return it, with his objections to that House in which it shall have originated, who shall enter the objections at large on their journal, and proceed to reconsider it. If after such reconsideration two thirds of that House shall agree to pass the bill, it shall be sent, together with the objections, to the other House, by which it shall likewise be reconsidered, and if approved by two thirds of that House, it shall become a law.

3. How can the members of Congress override the President's veto?

   Congress can override the President's veto through

   (1) unanimous approval from the House in which the bill originated
   (2) approval from two-thirds of the House in which the bill originated
   (3) changing the portions of the bill to which the President objected
   (4) gaining approval from the Speaker of the House of Representatives and the Vice President
   (5) approval from two-thirds of both Houses

4. Which of the following bills could not originate in the Senate?

   The Senate could not originate a bill that

   (1) establishes new federal education standards
   (2) institutes a higher tax on gasoline
   (3) changes the nation's health care system
   (4) places stricter emissions standards on automobiles
   (5) provides additional financial aid to college students

Questions 5 and 6 refer to the following excerpt.

From the Bill of Rights of the U.S. Constitution:

Amendment IX
   The enumeration in the Constitution, of certain rights, shall not be construed to deny or disparage others retained by the people.

5. Which of the following offers the best interpretation of Amendment IX?

   (1) The Constitution cannot be used to deny citizens their rights.
   (2) The United States government has inherent powers that are not described in the Constitution.
   (3) Each state has the authority to delegate rights to its citizens.
   (4) The fact that the Constitution describes certain rights does not mean that citizens do not have additional rights.
   (5) Citizens do not have the right to speak out against the provisions in the Bill of Rights.

6. What might activists use the Ninth Amendment to support?

   Activists may use the amendment to support the right

   (1) to legally own assault weapons
   (2) to privacy
   (3) to prohibit prayer in school
   (4) of defendants not to testify in court
   (5) of citizens to publically disagree with government policies

Analyze Information Sources

① Learn the Skill

When learning about social studies, you will often be required to **analyze** many different types of **information sources**. **Primary sources** are original accounts of events written by people who actually experienced them at the time, like an eyewitness. These sources include speeches, documents, journal entries, and letters. **Secondary sources** interpret primary sources. Encyclopedias, newspaper articles, and history books are secondary sources. It is important to distinguish between primary and secondary sources to understand the author's purpose and point of view. Remember that all sources have a degree of **bias**, or partiality. Be sure to evaluate sources critically.

② Practice the Skill

By mastering the skill of analyzing information sources, you will improve your study and test-taking skills, especially as they relate to the GED Social Studies Test. Read the excerpt and strategies below. Then answer the question that follows.

A The language of this question and the repetition of the phrase "I think" suggest that this passage expresses the author's beliefs and opinions. If people are trying to promote something, it could be said that they have a bias towards it. If against something, then they are biased against it.

B Titles, labels, captions, and so on can provide valuable information for evaluating a source.

> How many of you who are going to be doctors are willing to spend your days in Ghana? Technicians or engineers: how many of you are willing to work in the Foreign Service and spend your lives traveling around the world? On your willingness to do that, not merely to serve one year or two years in the service, but on your willingness to contribute part of your life to this country, I think will depend the answer whether a free society can compete. I think it can. And I think Americans are willing to contribute. But the effort must be far greater than we've ever made in the past.
>
> **B**
> From John F. Kennedy, Campaign Speech in Ann Arbor, Michigan, 1960

✓ TEST-TAKING TIPS

All sources have a degree of bias. Most scholarly works (secondary sources) attempt to prove a historical thesis, such as the role of economics during the American Revolution, and have to acknowledge the bias in the primary sources they use.

1. How does this excerpt show bias?

   Kennedy is biased towards

   (1) service programs
   (2) politics
   (3) doctors
   (4) Americans
   (5) engineers

Directions: Choose the one best answer to each question.

Questions 2 and 3 refer to the following excerpt.

Functions

The Supreme Court has two fundamental functions. On the one hand, it must interpret and expound all congressional enactments brought before it in proper cases; in this respect its role parallels that of the state courts of final resort in making the decisive interpretation of state law. On the other hand, the Supreme Court has power (superseding that of all other courts) to examine federal and state statutes and executive actions to determine whether they conform to the U.S. Constitution. When the court rules against the constitutionality of a statute or an executive action, its decision can be overcome only if the Constitution is amended or if the court later overrules itself or modifies its previous opinion.

From Columbia Encyclopedia article "Supreme Court, United States," 2001–2007

2. The information found in this source would be most like that found in which of the following?

(1) an interview
(2) a diary
(3) a speech
(4) a biography
(5) a historical document

3. How would you describe the information found in this source?

The information provided by this source is

(1) biased
(2) impassioned
(3) balanced
(4) dated
(5) incorrect

Questions 4 and 5 refer to the following graph.

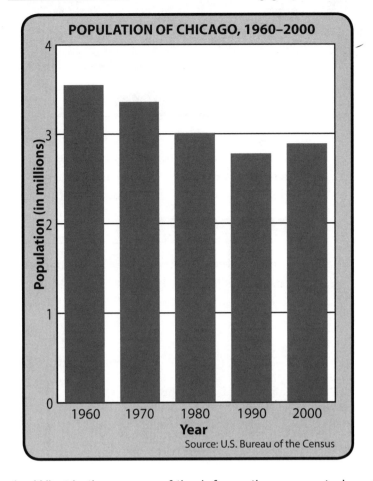

POPULATION OF CHICAGO, 1960–2000

Population (in millions) / Year

Source: U.S. Bureau of the Census

4. What is the source of the information presented in this graph?

(1) a corporation
(2) the city of Chicago
(3) a federal government agency
(4) an encyclopedia
(5) a national magazine

5. Which of the following is an example of a biased interpretation of this graph?

(1) The population of Chicago has declined over time.
(2) The decline in population was caused by an increase in violence by poor people.
(3) Chicago's population was higher in 1960 than it was in 2000.
(4) The population of Chicago has been declining over several decades for many reasons.
(5) The population of Chicago is not, in fact, declining.

Identify Problem and Solution

① Learn the Skill

Each day, people work to solve **problems** in their homes, schools, workplaces, and communities. The first step in solving a problem is to correctly identify and understand the problem in order to determine the best way to solve it. When determining a **solution**, it is important to identify a number of potential alternatives and evaluate the advantages and disadvantages of each.

② Practice the Skill

By mastering the skill of identifying problems and solutions, you will improve your study and test-taking skills, especially as they relate to the GED Social Studies Test. Read the excerpt and strategies below. Then answer the question that follows.

A In this passage, Treasury Secretary Henry Paulson describes an economic problem. Examine the details and examples Paulson gives to clearly explain the problem.

B In this section, Paulson attempts to describe a solution to this problem. Do you think Paulson believes this solution will be simple?

USING LOGIC

When reading about social studies, the text may not specifically state both the problem and solution in a given situation. You must often use the information provided about a problem to make inferences about possible solutions, and vice versa.

A The underlying weakness in our financial system today is the illiquid mortgage assets that have lost value as the housing correction has proceeded. These illiquid assets are choking off the flow of credit that is so vitally important to our economy. When the financial system works as it should, money and capital flow to and from households and businesses to pay for home loans, school loans and investments that create jobs. As illiquid mortgage assets block the system, the clogging of our financial markets has the potential to have significant effects on our financial system and our economy.

B … The federal government must implement a program to remove these illiquid assets that are weighing down our financial institutions and threatening our economy. … First, to provide critical additional funding to our mortgage markets … Second, to increase the availability of capital for new home loans … These two steps will provide some initial support to mortgage assets, but they are not enough.

From Statement by Treasury Secretary Henry M. Paulson, September 19, 2008

1. What is the main problem in this excerpt?

   (1) home loans
   (2) illiquid assets
   (3) mortgage markets
   (4) school loans
   (5) the capitalist system

Directions: Choose the <u>one best answer</u> to each question.

Questions 2 and 3 refer to the following excerpt.

In order to assure that an increasing population, accompanied by expanding settlement and growing mechanization, does not occupy and modify all areas within the United States and its possessions, leaving no lands designated for preservation and protection in their natural condition, it is hereby declared to be the policy of the Congress to secure for the American people of present and future generations the benefit of an enduring resource of wilderness. For this purpose there is hereby established a National Wilderness Preservation System to be composed of federally owned areas designated by Congress as 'wilderness areas', and these shall be administered for the use and enjoyment of the American people in such manner as will leave them unimpaired for future use and enjoyment as wilderness …

From *The Wilderness Act of 1964*

2. What problem is outlined in this excerpt?

   This excerpt describes the problem of

   (1) deforestation for the lumber industry
   (2) habitat loss for endangered wildlife
   (3) financial complications from logging regulations
   (4) overcrowding in U.S. urban areas
   (5) loss of wilderness due to increasing growth and development

3. How does this legislation propose to solve the problem?

   (1) creating new national parks
   (2) establishing protected wilderness areas
   (3) limiting the number of trees that can be cut down in U.S. forests
   (4) protecting several species of wildlife
   (5) building small communities in wilderness areas

Questions 4 and 5 refer to the following excerpt.

Section 1. No person shall be elected to the office of the President more than twice, and no person who has held the office of President, or acted as President, for more than two years of a term to which some other person was elected President shall be elected to the office of the President more than once. But this article shall not apply to any person holding the office of President when this article was proposed by the Congress, and shall not prevent any person who may be holding the office of President, or acting as President, during the term within which this article becomes operative from holding the office of President or acting as President during the remainder of such term.

From The United States Constitution, Amendment XXII (1951)

4. This amendment proposes a solution. What problem is it designed to address?

   (1) an unclear order of succession to the presidency
   (2) the increasing power of the executive branch
   (3) the contested election of the current President
   (4) the lack of term limits for the presidency
   (5) disputes between the President and Congress

5. Which historical event likely prompted the creation of this amendment?

   The creation of this amendment was likely prompted by

   (1) the assassination of President John F. Kennedy
   (2) President Richard Nixon's resignation
   (3) Franklin Delano Roosevelt's presidency
   (4) Gerald Ford's presidency
   (5) the election of Lyndon B. Johnson

Special-Purpose Maps

① Learn the Skill

Special-purpose maps share many similarities with political maps. Both types of maps show political boundaries such as cities, states, regions, and countries. However, special-purpose maps show additional features that do not appear on simple political maps. These features may include things such as congressional districts, products and resources, and the use of symbols to represent key elements.

② Practice the Skill

By mastering the skill of interpreting special-purpose maps, you will improve your study and test-taking skills, especially as they relate to the GED Social Studies Test. Examine the map and strategies below. Then answer the question that follows.

A This map shows political features typically associated with a political map. The political features on the map include the boundaries of the United States, as well as the locations of cities in which the branches of the Federal Reserve are located.

B In addition to these political features, however, the map also indicates the boundaries of the twelve Federal Reserve districts in the United States. The addition of this extra layer of information makes this visual a special-purpose map.

U.S. FEDERAL RESERVE DISTRICTS

9   Minneapolis
Chicago
7   2   Boston   1
12   Cleveland   3   New York
Kansas City   4   Philadelphia
San Francisco   10   St. Louis
  8   5   Richmond
B   11   6   Atlanta   **A**
Dallas

Alaska and Hawaii
are part of the
San Francisco District

☑ TEST-TAKING TIPS

When interpreting special-purpose maps in a test-taking situation, study the map's title and contents to identify the purpose the map will serve. Try to summarize this purpose in a sentence or two.

1. In which Federal Reserve district is the state of Texas located?

Texas is located in the

(1) 5ᵗʰ District
(2) 8ᵗʰ District
(3) 10ᵗʰ District
(4) 11ᵗʰ District
(5) 12ᵗʰ District

UNIT 4

③ Apply the Skill

Directions: Choose the one best answer to each question.

Questions 2 and 3 refer to the following map.

POPULATION OF GREAT LAKES STATES, 2000

👤 1 million people

2. Which state in this region had the largest population in 2000?

   (1) Ohio
   (2) Illinois
   (3) Michigan
   (4) Wisconsin
   (5) Minnesota

3. Which of the following statements is correct based on the information on the map?

   In 2000,

   (1) Minnesota had less than 5 million people
   (2) Wisconsin had a larger population than Indiana
   (3) Ohio and Michigan had a combined population of more than 20 million people
   (4) the two most populous states shared a border
   (5) the population of Illinois began to decrease

Questions 4 and 5 refer to the following map.

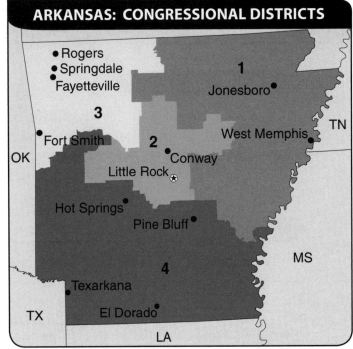

ARKANSAS: CONGRESSIONAL DISTRICTS

4. How are the Congressional districts shown on this map alike?

   Each of the Congressional districts shown on this map has approximately the same

   (1) area
   (2) number of large cities
   (3) population
   (4) appraised land value
   (5) types of industries

5. Why does Arkansas have 4 congressional districts?

   (1) It is the fourth largest state.
   (2) It has the fourth smallest population.
   (3) It is the population of Arkansas divided by total members of the U.S. Congress.
   (4) That is the number assigned to Arkansas by the U.S. House of Representatives when Arkansas was first made a state.
   (5) That is the number apportioned to Arkansas based on state population and the total number of U.S. Representatives.

Fact and Opinion

① Learn the Skill

A **fact** is a statement that can be proven true or untrue, while an **opinion** is a view or belief that cannot be proven true or untrue. Many times when reading about social studies, you will encounter statements of fact and opinion. The ability to distinguish between these two types of statements will enable you to better assess the accuracy of the information you read and determine how it relates to the subject you are studying.

② Practice the Skill

By mastering the skill of identifying fact and opinion, you will improve your study and test-taking skills, especially as they relate to the GED Social Studies Test. Read the excerpt and strategies below. Then answer the question that follows.

A Strongly worded or emotional sentiments such as these provide clues to the reader that the speaker or author is expressing an opinion.

B In these examples, the speaker uses statistical evidence that can be proven true or untrue. In social studies, facts are often used to support or discredit arguments.

A <u>We can't stand pat because it is essential with the conflict that we have around the world, that we not just hold our own</u>; that we not keep just freedom for ourselves. It is essential that we extend freedom—extend it to all the world. And this means more than what we've been doing. …

Now, looking at other parts of the world: South America, talking about our record and the previous one; we had a good neighbor policy, yes. It sounded fine. But let's look at it. <u>There were 11 dictators when we came into power in 1953 in Latin America. There are only three left</u>.

Let's look at Africa. <u>Twenty new countries in Africa during the course of this administration. Not one of them selected a Communist government</u>. All of them voted for freedom—a free type of government.

From Richard Nixon's remarks during the October 21, 1960 Presidential Debate

USING LOGIC

If you can name a piece of evidence that could logically prove a statement true, it is likely a fact. For opinions, you should not be able to think of pieces of evidence that could undeniably prove them true or false.

1. Which of the following ideas in Nixon's remarks expresses an opinion?

   (1) The Eisenhower administration's Latin American policy was called a good neighbor policy.
   (2) Twenty new countries emerged in Africa during the Eisenhower administration.
   (3) The United States should extend its freedom to the world.
   (4) Numerous dictators left power during the Eisenhower administration.
   (5) No new Communist governments were established in Africa.

UNIT 4

Directions: Choose the <u>one best answer</u> to each question.

<u>Questions 2 and 3</u> refer to the following information.

A debate has grown in the United States among defenders and critics of the Electoral College system. Some critics contend that this system has become outdated as the U.S. government has changed. Political leaders originally planned for the nation's government to take the form of a republic in which citizens elected officials to govern for them. Over time, though, the government has evolved into a democracy in which these officials are expected to govern according to the wishes of the people.

Additionally, critics argue that the Electoral College can allow a candidate to win the presidency while losing the popular vote. This has occurred during three presidential elections. Critics believe that this thwarts the will of the majority.

2. Which of the following is a fact that a defender of the Electoral College might cite to support his or her position?

   (1) The Electoral College has only failed to select the winner of the popular vote three times.
   (2) The Electoral College gives additional representation to smaller states.
   (3) The Electoral College was established many years ago.
   (4) Abolishing the Electoral College would destabilize the U.S. political system.
   (5) The Electoral College is necessary to preserve a two-party system.

3. What is one of the main opinions of Electoral College critics?

   Critics of the Electoral College believe that the system is

   (1) biased
   (2) fraught with corruption
   (3) controlled by a single party
   (4) no longer needed
   (5) too expensive

<u>Questions 4 and 5</u> refer to the following campaign poster from the 1944 presidential election.

4. Why would campaign posters like this one be likely to feature opinions?

   (1) to publicize the beliefs of experts
   (2) to appeal to the emotions of voters
   (3) to intimidate opposing candidates
   (4) to confuse electoral college members
   (5) to promote candidates' platforms

5. Which fact might an opponent use to refute the opinions on this poster?

   (1) Roosevelt had taken the country into World War II.
   (2) Roosevelt had physical handicaps.
   (3) Roosevelt was 62 years old in 1944.
   (4) Roosevelt had already served three terms as President.
   (5) Truman replaced Roosevelt's previous vice president.

Faulty Logic or Reasoning

① Learn the Skill

In Unit 3, you learned that generalizations are broad statements that apply to an entire group of people, things, or events. You also learned that these generalizations are considered invalid if they are not supported by facts. Such a generalization is also known as a **hasty generalization** and is an example of **faulty logic or reasoning**. You can find more information about logic and reasoning on pp. x–xiii.

② Practice the Skill

By mastering the skill of discerning faulty logic or reasoning, you will improve your study and test-taking skills, especially as they relate to the GED Social Studies Test. Read the excerpt and strategies below. Then answer the question that follows.

A Statements that make absolute or universal claims often exhibit faulty logic or reasoning. Because these statements can be disproven with a single piece of conflicting evidence, it makes it easier to highlight the faulty logic or reasoning used to make them.

B This statement provides another example of an absolute or universal claim ("no forces capable") that may be unlikely to hold up under close scrutiny.

> To the accusation that Cuba wants to export its revolution, we reply: <u>Revolutions are not exported, they are made by the people</u> … **A**
>
> What Cuba can give to the people, and has already given, is its example.
>
> And what does the Cuban Revolution teach? That revolution is possible, that the people can make it, that <u>in the contemporary world there are no forces capable of halting the liberation movement of the peoples</u>. **B**
>
> Our triumph would never have been feasible if the Revolution itself had not been inexorably destined to arise out of existing conditions in our socio-economic reality, a reality which exists to an even greater degree in a good number of Latin American countries.
>
> From Fidel Castro's "On the Export of Revolution"

⬛ MAKING ASSUMPTIONS

You can usually assume that an author or speaker uses reasoning and logic in order to explain some idea. When looking for faulty logic or reasoning, focus on statements that support the author or speaker's main ideas. Then, narrow your focus to those examples that appear to make unsupportable claims.

1. Which of the following would reveal the underlined claim in the third paragraph as an example of faulty reasoning?

   (1) a free election in Cuba
   (2) the removal of Castro from power
   (3) the military defeat of a liberation movement in Asia
   (4) United States support for liberation movements around the world
   (5) the outbreak of civil war in Cuba

UNIT 4

Directions: Choose the <u>one best answer</u> to each question.

Questions 2 and 3 refer to the following excerpt.

Whereas the successful prosecution of the war requires every possible protection against espionage and against sabotage to national-defense material, national-defense premises, and national-defense utilities … .I hereby authorize and direct the Secretary of War … to prescribe military areas in such places and of such extent as he or the appropriate Military Commanders may determine, from which any or all persons may be excluded, and with such respect to which, the right of any person to enter, remain in, or leave shall be subject to whatever restrictions the Secretary of War or the appropriate Military Commander may impose in his discretion.

From *Executive Order 9066*, issued by President Franklin D. Roosevelt, February 19, 1942

2. Which of the following groups of people were affected by this executive order?

   (1) Japanese Americans during World War II
   (2) German Americans during World War I
   (3) Spanish Americans during the Spanish-American War
   (4) Loyalists during the American Revolution
   (5) Russian Americans during World War II

3. Which of the following best expresses the hasty generalization made in this executive order?

   (1) All periods of wartime require citizens to give up personal freedoms.
   (2) All Military Commanders should receive absolute authority during times of war.
   (3) The President can never establish military areas.
   (4) All people whose ancestry traces to an enemy nation are worthy of suspicion.
   (5) Individuals imprisoned in military camps should always receive food and other important accommodations.

Question 4 refers to the following information and political cartoon.

Boris Pasternak was an acclaimed poet and author from the Soviet Union. His 1956 novel *Doctor Zhivago* criticized communism, and Soviet publishers refused to publish it. Pasternak received the 1958 Nobel Prize for literature for the novel. However, Soviet leaders would not permit him to travel in order to receive the award.

"I WON THE NOBEL PRIZE FOR LITERATURE. WHAT WAS YOUR CRIME?" by Bill Mauldin. Published in the *St. Louis Post-Dispatch*, October 30, 1958

4. The cartoon criticizes the faulty reasoning of the Soviet government.

   Based on the information, which of the following oversimplifications does the cartoonist criticize?

   (1) All criminals should be treated the same way.
   (2) All travel outside the Soviet Union should be forbidden.
   (3) All authors should be regarded with suspicion.
   (4) All criticism of the government should be treated as a crime.
   (5) All publishers should be controlled by the government.

Evaluate Information

① Learn the Skill

Just as you have learned to analyze information sources, you will also need to evaluate the information that you find in these various sources. **Evaluating information** requires you to closely examine information for purpose, bias, faulty logic and reasoning, and facts or opinions in order to make judgments about its quality. This skill combines many of the skills you have learned previously.

② Practice the Skill

By mastering the skill of evaluating information, you will improve your study and test-taking skills, especially as they relate to the GED Social Studies Test. Read the excerpt and strategies below. Then answer the question that follows.

A In this sentence, the commercial makes the claim that the job of California's governor is the nation's "second biggest," aside from the job of President. Claims such as this one can help you evaluate whether the information presented in a source is valid.

B The commercial cites a claim made by a newspaper regarding Reagan's record as governor of California. How does the description differ from the actual text in the newspaper? How does this show bias?

TEST-TAKING TIPS

Evaluating information requires you to assess a text for numerous characteristics. You may find it useful to preview the questions you will have to answer. This will allow you to narrow your focus as you begin to read and evaluate the text.

From Ronald Reagan television campaign commercial "Reagan's Record," 1980:

MALE NARRATOR: This is a man whose time has come. A strong leader with a proven record. In 1966, answering the class of his party, Ronald Reagan was elected Governor of California—<u>next to President, the biggest job in the nation</u>. What the new Governor inherited was a state of crisis. California was faced with a $194 million deficit and was spending a million dollars a day more than it was taking in. The state was on the brink of bankruptcy. Governor Reagan became the greatest tax reformer in the state's history. When Governor Reagan left office, the $194 million deficit had been transformed into a $550 million dollar surplus. <u>The San Francisco Chronicle said Governor Reagan has saved the state from bankruptcy</u>.

B [TEXT] 'We exaggerate very little when we say that [Reagan] has saved the state from bankruptcy.' –San Francisco Chronicle]

MALE NARRATOR: The time is now for strong leadership. [TEXT] Reagan for President.

1. Which of the following best describes the claims made in this commercial?

   (1) entirely valid
   (2) slightly exaggerated
   (3) falsified
   (4) entirely unsupported
   (5) greatly exaggerated

UNIT 4

Directions: Choose the one best answer to each question.

Questions 2 and 3 refer to the following excerpt.

In 1996, America will choose the President who will lead us from the millennium which saw the birth of our nation, and into a future that has all the potential to be even greater than our magnificent past. ...

Opportunity. Responsibility. Community. These are the values that made America strong. These are the values of the Democratic Party. These are the values that must guide us into the future.

Today, America is moving forward with the strong Presidential leadership it deserves. The economy is stronger, the deficit is lower, and government is smaller. Education is better, our environment is cleaner, families are healthier, and our streets are safer. There is more opportunity in America, more responsibility in our homes, and more peace in the world.

From the Democratic Party Platform of 1996

2. What was the purpose of the information in this excerpt?

   The information in the excerpt was designed

   (1) to provide details about new policies supported by Democrats
   (2) to foster a sense of well-being and to encourage the reelection of Bill Clinton
   (3) to gain support for new health care policies
   (4) to defend the Democratic Party against charges leveled by the Republicans
   (5) to look forward to the year 2000

3. Which of the following claims made in this excerpt could be most easily supported?

   (1) There is more responsibility in our homes.
   (2) There is more peace in the world.
   (3) There is more opportunity in America.
   (4) The deficit is lower.
   (5) Families are healthier.

Questions 4 and 5 refer to the following excerpt.

On domestic issues, the choice is also clear. In critical areas such as public education and health care, Bush's emphasis is on greater competition. His No Child Left Behind Act has flaws, but its requirements have created a new climate of expectation and accountability. On both of these important fronts, but especially with his expensive health-care plan, Kerry primarily sees a need to raise and spend more money. ...

John Kerry has been a discerning critic of where Bush has erred. But Kerry's message—a more restrained assault on global threats, earnest comfort with the international community's noble inaction— suggests what many voters sense: After 20 years in the Senate, the moral certitude Kerry once displayed has evaporated. There is no landmark Kennedy-Kerry Education Act, no Kerry-Frist Health Bill. Today's Kerry is more about plans and process than solutions. He is better suited to analysis than to action. He has not delivered a compelling blueprint for change.

From the *Chicago Tribune*: "George W. Bush for president" 2004

4. Which of the following does the author cite in order to validate an endorsement of one candidate's domestic policies?

   (1) Bush's landmark health care plan
   (2) the No Child Left Behind Act
   (3) the Kennedy-Kerry Education Act
   (4) the Kerry-Frist Health Bill
   (5) Bush's assault on global threats

5. What is the main purpose of this editorial?

   This editorial was designed

   (1) to explain why the writer voted for John Kerry
   (2) to explain why the writer voted for George W. Bush
   (3) to convince voters that John Kerry's policies were failures
   (4) to convince voters that George W. Bush's policies were successful
   (5) to convince people to vote for George W. Bush

Analyze Effectiveness of Arguments

① Learn the Skill

In reading texts, particularly those focusing on social studies material, you will often need to **identify strong and weak arguments**. A strong argument is persuasive and backed by accurate sources. On the other hand, a weak argument lacks the factual support needed to make it convincing. In order to **analyze the effectiveness of an argument**, look for the supporting evidence that the author or speaker provides and consider whether it is convincing.

② Practice the Skill

By mastering the skill of analyzing the effectiveness of arguments, you will improve your study and test-taking skills, especially as they relate to the GED Social Studies Test. Read the excerpt and strategies below. Then answer the question that follows.

A The arguments made in this excerpt follow a repeating pattern. How does the repetition of this pattern make the argument more or less effective?

B The speaker continues to draw distinctions between his proposals and those of his opponent. What support could be offered for these arguments in order to make them more convincing?

> I will keep taxes low and cut them where I can. My opponent will raise them. I will open new markets to our goods and services. My opponent will close them. I will cut government spending. He will increase it.
>
> My tax cuts will create jobs. His tax increases will eliminate them. My health care plan will make it easier for more Americans to find and keep good health care insurance. His plan will force small businesses to cut jobs, reduce wages, and force families into a government run health care system where a bureaucrat stands between you and your doctor.
>
> From John McCain's address accepting the Republican Party Presidential Nomination, September 4, 2008

✓ TEST-TAKING TIPS

When analyzing the effectiveness of an argument, you should first try to formulate a brief summary of the argument that the author is trying to make. With this summary in mind, you can then look more closely at the supporting details provided in order to assess the effectiveness of the argument.

1. McCain argues that his economic and health care proposals will be more effective than those of his opponent.

   Which of the following would strengthen McCain's argument?

   (1) additional details about his efforts to reform health care as a Senator
   (2) reflections on Democratic and Republican views about taxes
   (3) data from both candidates' proposed federal budgets
   (4) a list of Democratic Presidents who have increased taxes
   (5) an anecdote about a struggling small business in the United States

Directions: Choose the <u>one best answer</u> to each question.

Questions 2 and 3 refer to the following excerpt.

Senator William Fulbright: As I stated, section I is intended to deal primarily with aggression against our forces … . I do not know what the limits are. I do not think this resolution can be determinative of that fact. I think it would indicate that he [President Johnson] would take reasonable means first to prevent any further aggression, or repel further aggression against our own forces … . I do not know how to answer the Senator's question and give him an absolute assurance that large numbers of troops would not be put ashore. I would deplore it … .

Senator Ernest Gruening: Regrettably, I find myself in disagreement with the President's Southeast Asian policy … The serious events of the past few days, the attack by North Vietnamese vessels on American warships and our reprisal, strikes me as the inevitable and foreseeable concomitant and consequence of U.S. unilateral military aggressive policy in Southeast Asia … . We now are about to authorize the President if he sees fit to move our Armed Forces … not only into South Vietnam, but also into North Vietnam, Laos, Cambodia, Thailand, and of course the authorization includes all the rest of the SEATO nations … . This resolution is a further authorization for escalation unlimited. I am opposed to sacrificing a single American boy in this venture. We have lost far too many already … .

From Senate Debates on the Tonkin Gulf Resolution, August 6–7, 1964

2. Which of the following does Fulbright use to support his argument?

 (1) statistics regarding the conflict in Vietnam
 (2) details about the meaning of the resolution
 (3) his beliefs about the President's intent
 (4) recommendations from foreign policy experts
 (5) testimony from military leaders

3. What is the argument made by Senator Gruening in this excerpt?

 Senator Gruening argues that

 (1) the resolution will lead to unchecked U.S. aggression in Southeast Asia
 (2) the resolution will enable the United States to defend its forces overseas
 (3) the North Vietnamese attack on U.S. forces was unprovoked
 (4) the United States should devote more troops to preserving peace in Asia
 (5) the President would not use the resolution to wage war in other parts of the world

Question 4 refers to the following excerpt.

 You see, we Democrats have a very different measure of what constitutes progress in this country.

 We measure progress by how many people can find a job that pays the mortgage; whether you can put a little extra money away at the end of each month so you can someday watch your child receive her college diploma. We measure progress in the 23 million new jobs that were created when Bill Clinton was President—when the average American family saw its income go up $7,500 instead of down $2,000 like it has under George Bush.

From Barack Obama's address accepting the Democratic Party Presidential Nomination, August 28, 2008

4. How does Obama best strengthen his argument that Democrats can improve the nation's economy?

 (1) He refutes the economic gains of the sitting Republican administration.
 (2) He describes his definition of the word progress.
 (3) He details a plan for college savings.
 (4) He cites the economic improvements of the last Democratic administration.
 (5) He cites the number of billionaires in the nation and lists successful corporations.

UNIT 4

Unit 4 Review

The Unit Review is structured to resemble the GED Social Studies Test. Be sure to read each question and all possible answers very carefully before choosing your answer.

To record your answers, fill in the numbered circle that corresponds to the answer you select for each question in the Unit Review.

Do not rest your pencil on the answer area while considering your answer. Make no stray or unnecessary marks. If you change an answer, erase your first mark completely.

Mark only one answer space for each question; multiple answers will be scored as incorrect.

Sample Question

Which of the following accurately describes the contents of the U. S. Constitution?

(1) articles
(2) articles and amendments
(3) articles, amendments, and bills
(4) articles, amendments, bills, and check and balances
(5) articles, amendments, bills, checks and balances, and three branches of government

① ● ③ ④ ⑤

Directions: Choose the one best answer to each question.

Questions 1 and 2 refer to the following table.

1992 PRESIDENTIAL ELECTION RESULTS			
CANDIDATE (PARTY)	ELECTORAL VOTES (%)	POPULAR VOTES (%)	STATES WON
Bill Clinton (Democratic)	370 (68.8%)	44,909,326 (43.0%)	32 (also won Washington, D.C.)
George H.W. Bush (Republican)	168 (31.2%)	39,103,882 (37.4%)	18
H. Ross Perot (Independent)	0 (0%)	19,741,657 (18.9%)	0

1. Which of the following statements about the table expresses an opinion?

(1) Clinton won both the electoral vote and the popular vote.
(2) If Perot had not entered the election, Bush would have been reelected as President.
(3) Bush won similar percentages of the popular and electoral votes.
(4) Despite receiving almost 20 million popular votes, Perot did not receive a vote in the Electoral College.
(5) Bush received approximately double the number of popular votes Perot received.

① ② ③ ④ ⑤

2. Suppose you are assigned to write a research report on the Presidential election of 1992. What primary sources might you consult in order to learn more about the results shown in the table?

You might consult a primary source such as

(1) a newspaper article about the election
(2) an American history textbook
(3) a biography of Perot
(4) an encyclopedia entry on political parties
(5) an interview of one of the candidates' campaign managers

① ② ③ ④ ⑤

Questions 3 and 4 refer to the following information.

In the United States, affirmative action programs have been designed to create greater opportunities for underrepresented minority groups in areas such as the workplace, college admissions, and the issuing of government contracts. The policies have been instituted with the intent of offsetting the harmful effects of past discrimination.

Affirmative action has proven to be highly controversial in the United States. Opponents argue that these policies violate citizens' right to equal protection by the nation's laws. They further claim that discriminating against members of a present-day group to make amends for past discrimination against a different group is unfair.

Supporters of affirmative action counter that people experience discrimination specifically because they belong to a particular group. As a result, they believe it is necessary to institute systematic measures to guarantee that equal rights remain **inviolable** for all citizens.

3. What problem have affirmative action programs been established to address?

   (1) the shortage of institutes of higher learning in the United States
   (2) the difficulty of interpreting cases involving equal protection disputes
   (3) conflicts arising between different ethnic and religious groups in U.S. communities
   (4) the harmful effects of past discrimination
   (5) the lack of high-paying jobs for many Americans

   ① ② ③ ④ ⑤

4. By using context clues, what can you determine about the meaning of the word *inviolable*?

   The meaning of the word *inviolable* is

   (1) involuntary
   (2) optional
   (3) safe from violation
   (4) transferable from one person to another
   (5) varied from person to person

   ① ② ③ ④ ⑤

Questions 5 and 6 refer to the following excerpt from Article IV of the United States Constitution.

Section 3. New states may be admitted by the Congress into this union; but no new states shall be formed or erected within the jurisdiction of any other state; nor any state be formed by the junction of two or more states, or parts of states, without the consent of the legislatures of the states concerned as well as of the Congress.

The Congress shall have power to dispose of and make all needful rules and regulations respecting the territory or other property belonging to the United States; and nothing in this Constitution shall be so construed as to prejudice any claims of the United States, or of any particular state.

Section 4. The United States shall guarantee to every state in this union a republican form of government, and shall protect each of them against invasion; and on application of the legislature, or of the executive (when the legislature cannot be **convened**) against domestic violence.

5. What is the main focus of Section 3 of Article IV of the United States Constitution?

   (1) federal protection of the states
   (2) the formation of new states
   (3) the negotiation of treaties between the states
   (4) the interactions of state and federal legislatures
   (5) the authority of Congress in territorial disputes

   ① ② ③ ④ ⑤

6. Use context clues to determine the meaning of the word *convened* in the above excerpt.

   In this excerpt, the meaning of *convened* is

   (1) meet
   (2) established
   (3) disbanded
   (4) vote
   (5) be elected

   ① ② ③ ④ ⑤

Questions 7 through 10 refer to the following excerpts.

BUSH: Well, I think one thing that distinguishes is experience. I think we've dramatically changed the world. I'll talk about that a little bit later, but the changes are mind-boggling for world peace. Kids go to bed at night without the same fear of nuclear war. And change for change's sake isn't enough. We saw that message in the late seventies when we heard a lot about change. And what happened? That 'misery index' went right through the roof.

But my economic program, I think, is the kind of change we want. And the way we're going to get it done is we're going to have a brand new Congress. A lot of them are thrown out because of all the scandals. I'll sit down with them, Democrats and Republicans alike, and work for my Agenda for American Renewal which represents real change. But I'd say, if you had to separate out, I think it's experience at this level.

CLINTON: I believe experience counts, but it's not everything. Values, judgment, and the record that I have amassed in my State also should count for something. I've worked hard to create good jobs and to educate people. My state now ranks first in the country in job growth this year, fourth in income growth, fourth in the reduction of poverty, third in overall economic performance, according to a major news magazine. That's because we believe in investing in education and in jobs… .

Experience is important, yes. I've gotten a lot of good experience in dealing with ordinary people over the last year and a month… . And I think the American people deserve better than they're getting. We have gone from first to 13th in the world in wages in the last 12 years since Mr. Bush and Mr. Reagan have been in. Personal income has dropped while people have worked harder in the last 4 years. There have been twice as many bankruptcies as new jobs created.

We need a new approach. The same old experience is not relevant. We're living in a new world after the Cold War… . And you can have the right kind of experience and the wrong kind of experience. Mine is rooted in the lives of real people. And it will bring real results if we have the courage to change.

From the Presidential Debate: St. Louis, October 11, 1992

7. Which of the following serves as the basis of Bush's argument in this excerpt?

   (1) his Presidential experience
   (2) his economic program
   (3) his expectations for changes in Congress
   (4) his knowledge of U.S. government history
   (5) his understanding of the "misery index"

   ①②③④⑤

8. Which best describes the way in which Bush claims to have solved a foreign policy problem?

   Bush suggests that his administration has

   (1) restored alliances with former allies
   (2) brought an end to many violent uprisings around the world
   (3) negotiated peace treaties between numerous warring nations
   (4) remained a neutral peacemaker in many important world conflicts
   (5) reduced the fear of nuclear war

   ①②③④⑤

9. How does Clinton strengthen his argument about his experience to lead the nation?

   Clinton strengthens his argument by including statistics about

   (1) his proposed economic initiatives
   (2) his budgetary planning experience
   (3) economic improvements in Arkansas during his tenure as governor
   (4) the impact of his proposed tax policy
   (5) the limited economic growth that occurred during the Bush administration

   ①②③④⑤

10. Which of Clinton's statements below presents a fact?

    (1) We need a new approach.
    (2) I think the American people deserve better than what they're getting.
    (3) I believe experience counts, but it's not everything.
    (4) There have been twice as many bankruptcies as new jobs created.
    (5) The same old experience is not relevant.

    ①②③④⑤

UNIT 4

Questions 11 and 12 refer to the following political cartoon.

THE PRE-PRIMARY VOTE

"THE PRE-PRIMARY VOTE,"
A 1999 Herblock Cartoon, © by The Herb Block Foundation

11. Which of the following best describes the problem to which the cartoonist is trying to draw attention?

    (1) a lack of qualified Presidential candidates
    (2) the unreliability of Presidential elections
    (3) the increasing importance of campaign fundraising in the electoral process
    (4) the unwillingness of Americans to financially support the candidates that share their ideas
    (5) the secretive manner in which parties encourage candidates to run for office
    ① ② ③ ④ ⑤

12. How would you evaluate this cartoon as an information source?

    As an information source, this cartoon could best be described as

    (1) impartial
    (2) unreliable
    (3) propaganda
    (4) commentary
    (5) factually accurate
    ① ② ③ ④ ⑤

Questions 13 and 14 refer to the following excerpt.

Immigration was broken before the candidates started this repugnant ad war, and looks as if it will stay that way for at least the duration of this campaign… .

Both candidates once espoused smart, thoughtful positions for fixing the problem. But Mr. McCain is shuffling in step with his restrictionist party. Mr. Obama gave immigration one brief mention at the Democratic convention, in a litany of big-trouble issues… on which he seemed to say that the best Americans could hope for are small compromises and to agree to disagree.

They're both wrong. The country needs to hear better answers, stated clearly and forthrightly over the shouting. The answer to immigration is what it was last year: comprehensive reform that extends order and the rule of law to a system that is broken in a million complex ways. Mr. McCain and Mr. Obama both know this. They should get back to telling the truth about it, in English and in Spanish.

New York Times Editorial, "Immigration Deception," September 19, 2008

13. Why should this editorial be respected?

    This editorial should be respected because it comes from

    (1) a reputable newspaper
    (2) a popular political magazine
    (3) a government web site
    (4) a television news program
    (5) a scholarly essay
    ① ② ③ ④ ⑤

14. What error in reasoning does the author suggest John McCain makes regarding his immigration policy?

    (1) He only briefly discusses the issue during his convention speech.
    (2) He changes his views to remain consistent with party leadership.
    (3) He seeks a small compromise rather than a proper solution.
    (4) He refuses to attack Obama's views on immigration.
    (5) He focuses on immigration as an important campaign issue.
    ① ② ③ ④ ⑤

Questions 15 and 16 refer to the following political cartoon.

"BY TH' WAY, WHAT'S THAT BIG WORD?"
by Bill Mauldin

15. How do the figures shown in this cartoon demonstrate faulty logic?

These figures demonstrate faulty logic because

(1) they cannot agree on the best method for testing voters
(2) they cannot justify their choices of selected candidates
(3) they have oversimplified the qualifications for voting
(4) they made a hasty generalization that only opposing party members would be affected by the literacy tests
(5) an honest literacy test would prevent them from voting

① ② ③ ④ ⑤

16. Under which of the following headings could this cartoon best be categorized?

(1) democratic reforms
(2) Presidential elections
(3) government spending
(4) civil rights
(5) the U.S. Constitution

① ② ③ ④ ⑤

Questions 17 and 18 refer to the following excerpt.

Twenty years ago, the economy was in shambles. Unemployment was at 7.1 percent, inflation at 13.5 percent, and interest rates at 15.3 percent. The Democratic Party accepted that malaise as the price the nation had to pay for Big Government, and in doing so lost the confidence of the American people. Inspired by Presidents Reagan and Bush, Republicans hammered into place the framework for today's prosperity and surpluses. We cut taxes, simplified the tax code, deregulated industries, and opened world markets to American enterprise. The result was the tremendous growth in the 1980s that created the venture capital to launch the technology revolution of the 1990s.

That's the origin of what is now called the New Economy: the longest economic boom in the Twentieth Century, 40 million new jobs, the lowest inflation and unemployment in memory.

From the Republican Party Platform of 2000

17. Which of the following claims is best supported by facts listed in the platform?

(1) Republicans were inspired by Reagan and Bush during the 1980s and early 1990s.
(2) Twenty years ago, the economy was in shambles.
(3) The Democratic Party viewed economic difficulties as a necessary consequence of Big Government.
(4) Republicans simplified the U.S. tax code.
(5) The U.S. economy experienced significant growth during the 1980s.

① ② ③ ④ ⑤

18. How does this party platform show bias?

(1) It explains the origins of the New Economy.
(2) It discusses the economic growth of the 1980s.
(3) President Clinton's accomplishments are not included.
(4) The technology revolution is attributed to the simplified tax code.
(5) Presidents Reagan and Bush are not discussed.

① ② ③ ④ ⑤

Questions 19 through 22 refer to the following map.

Before each Presidential election, news organizations use polling to track voter trends in each state. This map reflects data from mid-October 2008.

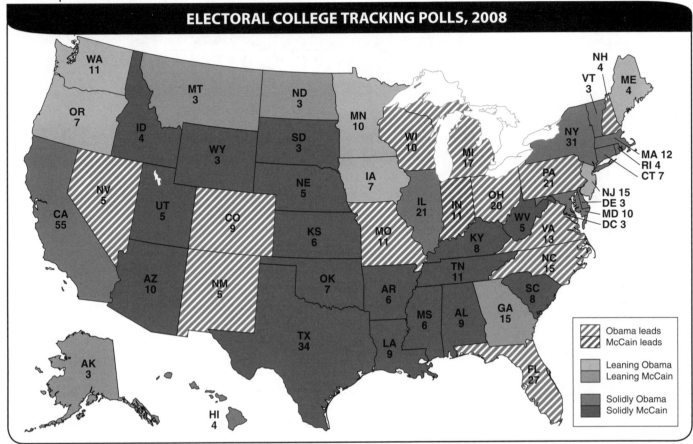

ELECTORAL COLLEGE TRACKING POLLS, 2008

19. What does the shading of Indiana mean?

The shading means that

(1) McCain leads in Indiana
(2) Obama leads in Indiana
(3) Indiana is leaning towards McCain
(4) Indiana is leaning towards Obama
(5) McCain has a solid lead in Indiana

①②③④⑤

20. This special-purpose map supports which of the following trends?

(1) The South was universally Republican.
(2) The Midwest was universally Democratic.
(3) Party loyalties were split along regional lines.
(4) Obama had at least some support in all regions of the country.
(5) McCain had the support of the most populous states.

①②③④⑤

21. If the presidential election would have been held that day, what would the result have been?

(1) McCain would have won the election.
(2) Obama would have won the election.
(3) There would have been a tie at 269 Electoral votes each.
(4) There is not enough data to determine the results.
(5) John McCain would have won more total states than Obama.

①②③④⑤

22. How did political pundits explain the fact that Obama was leading in traditionally Republican states such as North Carolina and Colorado?

(1) his race
(2) changing demographics
(3) population increases
(4) his running-mate
(5) McCain's age

①②③④⑤

DAVE THOMAS

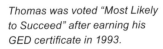

Dave Thomas's first love also led to his greatest regret. Thomas, the famed founder of Wendy's, the nation's third-largest restaurant chain, landed his first restaurant job at age 12. Three years later, he decided to leave school to work full-time at a restaurant in Fort Wayne, Indiana. He wouldn't return to school for another 45 years.

In between, Thomas experienced tremendous successes. He used the million dollars he earned from running four successful KFC franchises in 1966 to start his dream hamburger restaurant, Wendy's. In 1989, he appeared in the first of more than 800 Wendy's television commercials and, as a result, became one of America's most recognizable citizens. He noted,

> **Only in America would a guy like me, from humble beginnings and without a high school diploma, become successful.**

Thomas, however, believed in using his celebrity to aid important causes. In 1990, Thomas, himself an adopted child, was named by President Bush to lead the White House Initiative on Adoption. Two years later, he founded the Dave Thomas Foundation for Adoption, a non-profit organization that offers regional and national grants to raise awareness of adoption and to ease the process and its costs. He donated millions of dollars to research centers and hospitals.

A strong believer in education, Thomas established and supported business programs at Duke University in North Carolina and Nova University in Florida. Still, despite all of his successes, something was missing from Thomas's life. Thomas had left school at age 15. In 1993, he joined the class at Coconut Creek High School in Florida to earn his GED certificate and, in a nod to his career, was named "Most Likely to Succeed."

Thomas was voted "Most Likely to Succeed" after earning his GED certificate in 1993.

BIO BLAST: Dave Thomas

- Born in Atlantic City, New Jersey
- Opened first Wendy's in 1969 in Columbus, Ohio
- Served on White House Initiative for Adoption
- Donated millions of dollars to research centers and hospitals
- Authored multiple books, including *Dave's Way* and *Well Done!*
- Founded the Wellington School

Unit 5: Economics

Many of the choices we make each day revolve around economics. For example, we collect paychecks, make deposits and withdrawals, shop, and pay bills and taxes. Economics is the study of the decisions involved in the production, distribution, and consumption of goods and services. By understanding economics, we become better consumers about when and how we use our time and money.

Likewise, economics plays an important part in the GED Social Studies Test, comprising 20 percent of all questions. As with other parts of the GED Tests, economics will test your ability to interpret text and graphics using the thinking skills of comprehension, application, analysis, and evaluation. In Unit 5, the continuation of core skills and the introduction of others will help you prepare for the Social Studies Test.

Table of Contents

UNIT 5

Understand Economics

① Learn the Skill

Economics is the study of the ways in which goods and services are exchanged. It includes exchanges between people, groups, businesses, and governments. It borrows from human psychology, ethics, and history in its attempts to explain and predict behaviors related to buying and selling. Learning to **understand economics** is essential for making sense of societal behaviors and world events.

② Practice the Skill

By mastering the skill of understanding economics, you will improve your study and test-taking skills, especially as they relate to the GED Social Studies Test. Examine the cartoon and the information below. Then answer the question that follows.

"But on the bright side...we're holding our own in a ten trillion dollar economy!"

<u>Microeconomics</u> is the branch of economics that focuses on details, such as small groups of consumers and individual companies. It examines the needs of these groups and how they are satisfied.

<u>Macroeconomics</u> studies the bigger picture. It focuses on issues like national income, inflation, and employment rates. It is not always possible to distinguish between microeconomics and macroeconomics, since the two branches connect in a number of complex ways.

A The cartoon uses an image of a lemonade stand as a symbol of a small business.

B To help you remember the difference between micro- and macroeconomics, think that *micro* can mean small and *macro* is the opposite.

TEST-TAKING TIPS

Try to think of an example that illustrates any unfamiliar term or concept. For example, you might differentiate between micro- and macroeconomics by thinking about your personal spending habits versus the economic policies of the United States.

1. Which of the following sentences is true about the above cartoon?

   (1) It explains macroeconomics.
   (2) It illustrates a cause of inflation.
   (3) It defines the term "unemployment rate."
   (4) It lists sources of national income.
   (5) It illustrates a connection between microeconomics and macroeconomics.

UNIT 5

Directions: Choose the <u>one best answer</u> to each question.

<u>Questions 2 through 4</u> refer to the following information.

Adam Smith lived in Scotland during the time of America's Revolutionary War. In 1776, he published *The Wealth of Nations*. The book was the first to seriously examine the ways in which wealth is produced and distributed.

Smith believed that a country's economy works best when its government does not interfere with it. He asserted that when people were left to produce wealth without interference, they were led by an "invisible hand" to the benefit of all.

From Adam Smith's *The Wealth of Nations*:

The annual labour of every nation is the fund which originally supplies it with all the necessaries and conveniences of life which it annually consumes, and which consist always either in the immediate produce of that labor, or in what is purchased with that produce from other nations.

According therefore, as this produce, or what is purchased with it, bears a greater or smaller proportion to the number of those who are to consume it, the nation will be better or worse supplied with all the necessaries and conveniences for which it has occasion.

2. Which of the following is another way of expressing Smith's economic philosophy?

   The best economies are

   (1) planned economies
   (2) centralized economies
   (3) free market economies
   (4) government-controlled economies
   (5) socialist economies

3. According to Smith, which of the following can you infer should be a function of government?

   (1) to remove obstacles to business growth
   (2) to give people money to start businesses
   (3) to limit the profit a business can make
   (4) to restrict a business's hiring practices
   (5) to set the prices of goods and services

4. According to Smith, what produces a nation's wealth?

   (1) produce from other nations
   (2) the labor of its workforce
   (3) its necessaries
   (4) its luxuries
   (5) its proportion of necessaries to luxuries

<u>Questions 5 and 6</u> refer to the following information.

Capitalism, socialism, and communism are examples of economic systems. They vary by the amount of control the government or central authority has over businesses. The capitalist system has the least amount of government interference. The United States has a capitalist economic system.

Adam Smith and other economists favored a type of capitalism known as *laissez-faire*. This is a French term that means to let people do as they choose. In economics, it means that the government should not interfere. This theory was seen as inadequate by economist John Maynard Keynes. During the Great Depression, Keynes began to support the idea that government should make investments in society and businesses to spur the economy. Keynesian economists called for the same investment during the economic struggles of 2008–2009.

5. What type of economic system is most often practiced in the United States?

   (1) Keynesian capitalism
   (2) *laissez-faire* capitalism
   (3) socialism
   (4) *laissez-faire* socialism
   (5) communism

6. Why might Keynes have supported government investment during the Great Depression?

   Keynes believed that the United States government

   (1) should create jobs to lower unemployment
   (2) would cause private citizens not to invest in businesses
   (3) should run a deficit at all times
   (4) should follow the *laissez-faire* philosophy
   (5) would cure the recession by raising taxes

UNIT 5

Interpret Flowcharts

1 Learn the Skill

A flowchart is a graphic used to describe a sequence. It is a way to quickly communicate the steps of a process without using a lot of explanatory text. Learning to **interpret flowcharts** makes it easy to quickly grasp the information they convey. Flowcharts are similar to sequence charts, but their main focus is to illustrate a process instead of providing only a sequence of events.

2 Practice the Skill

By mastering the skill of interpreting flowcharts, you will improve your study and test-taking skills, especially as they relate to the GED Social Studies Test. Examine the information and the flowchart below. Then answer the question that follows.

The way in which businesses provide goods or services is called the production process.

A Flowcharts usually contain arrows to indicate the order of the sequence.

B Flowcharts are not always a simple line of boxes. A flow chart that demonstrates a cycle, for instance, might be circular.

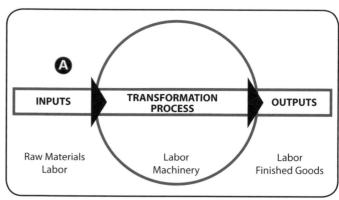

This flowchart is applicable to most businesses. For example, the input for a bakery is the labor, ovens, and ingredients needed to bake bread. After undergoing the transformation of mixing, baking, and packaging, the output is provided to the consumer.

MAKING ASSUMPTIONS

You can assume that labor is vital to almost all parts of the production process. Even if machines do a majority of the work, employees are necessary to operate and monitor the machines. Also, remember the labor involved in delivering, stocking, or selling a product.

1. Which of the following best describes the transformation process for a candle-making business?

   (1) purchasing string for wicks and blocks of wax, and hiring workers to run the melting machine
   (2) training workers to operate the melting machine
   (3) driving the trucks that deliver the candles
   (4) melting the wax, inserting the wicks, molding the wax, letting it cool
   (5) training workers to load trucks

Directions: Choose the <u>one best answer</u> to each question.

Questions 2 through 5 refer to the following flowchart and information.

PHASES OF A BUSINESS CYCLE

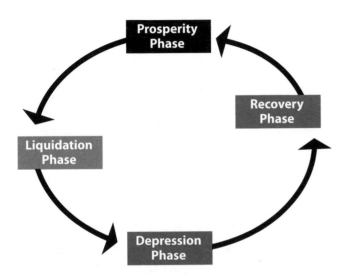

Economists use the term "business cycle" to describe recurring patterns of change in the economy. Although the specifics of a business cycle are not predictable, these four phases have been identified:

Prosperity phase: Businesses open and expand, production rises, profits increase, more money is invested, employment rate rises

Liquidation phase: Factors arise that make business less profitable, production drops, investment drops, employment drops

Depression phase: Businesses close, unemployment becomes widespread, little or no investment

Recovery phase: Factors arise that stimulate business, businesses open, investment resumes, employment rate rises

2. Where on the cycle would you expect to find the greatest number of families buying new homes?

    (1) during the liquidation phase
    (2) during the liquidation and depression phases
    (3) during the depression phase
    (4) during the recovery and prosperity phases
    (5) during the prosperity phase

3. Which of the following is necessary to move from a depression phase to a recovery phase?

    (1) a rise in unemployment
    (2) a stimulation of the economy
    (3) a drop in business profits
    (4) a decrease in investment
    (5) a slowdown in new business starts

4. The length of a prosperity phase is most associated with which of the following?

    (1) an extended decrease in production
    (2) a leveling-off in investment
    (3) a decline in new business starts
    (4) continued economic growth
    (5) an increase in unemployment

5. Which factors were the main causes for the recovery phase during the Great Depression?

    (1) the election of Franklin Roosevelt to four consecutive terms as President
    (2) banks failed and the stock market crashed
    (3) New Deal legislation and World War II
    (4) the founding of the WPA and high unemployment
    (5) the repeal of prohibition and a reduction in lending

Multiple Causes and Effects

① Learn the Skill

Not every cause-and-effect relationship is simple. Many causes can contribute to a single result, and a single event or situation may result in multiple effects. Knowing how to identify **multiple causes and effects** will help you form a complete understanding of the subject you are studying. It will help you be more aware of historical trends.

② Practice the Skill

By learning to identify multiple causes and effects, you will improve your study and test-taking skills, especially as they relate to the GED Social Studies Test. Examine the information and the bar graph below. Then answer the question that follows.

A Inflation causes a chain reaction of events, such as rising prices and fewer purchases.

B Inflation is the cause. Wars, problems with the food supply, and political unrest are some of the effects.

One important area of macroeconomic study is inflation. **A** Inflation occurs when the supply of money exceeds the goods and services available. This causes the value of the money to fall and prices to rise. This, in turn, discourages people from making purchases. The effects are felt in all sectors of the economy and all segments of society.

Inflation and the economic instability it spawns have been known to cause wars, problems in the food supply, and political unrest. Developing nations, such as those in Africa, are in the most danger from inflation.

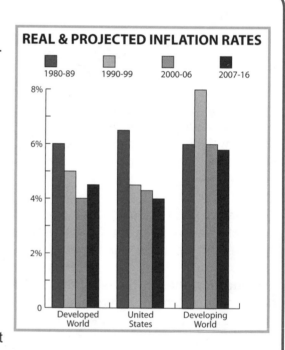

REAL & PROJECTED INFLATION RATES

1980-89   1990-99   2000-06   2007-16

MAKING ASSUMPTIONS

You might assume that having more money than can be spent is good for an economy. The information on this page explains why that is not true.

1. Which part of the world is most affected by inflation?

   (1) The United States is most affected.
   (2) The developing world is most affected.
   (3) The developed world is most affected.
   (4) All parts of the world economy are affected equally.
   (5) Few parts of the world show signs of inflation.

③ Apply the Skill

Directions: Choose the <u>one best answer</u> to each question.

<u>Questions 2 through 5</u> refer to the following graph and information.

The cause-and-effect relationship between supply and demand is a strong determing factor of prices.

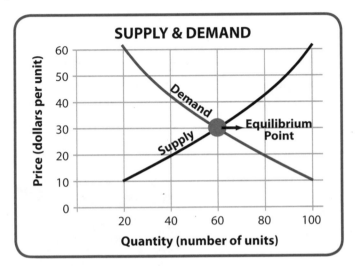

SUPPLY & DEMAND

According to the economic laws of supply and demand, people will pay more for something they want when less of it is available. On the other hand, if there is more of a supply of a good or service than people demand, the supplier will lower the price to coax people into buying more of it.

The point at which the price of an item and the amount of demand are the same is called the equilibrium point. At prices above the equilibrium point, demand drops. If the price becomes too high, demand may disappear completely. However, if the price becomes too low, the seller will be unable to make a profit and will stop producing the item.

Supply and demand are themselves the effects of other causes. For example, the effects of inflation can decrease demand and force down an item's price. Inflation can also raise the cost of producing an item, resulting in a higher price, which can also lead to a decrease in demand.

2. Which of the following statements is true?

   Supply, demand, and inflation

   (1) are each basic causes of economic activity
   (2) are each terms with no real definition
   (3) operate independently of one another
   (4) do not influence the economy
   (5) are each influenced by many causes

3. Based on the information, what needs to exist for the law of supply and demand to function freely?

   (1) competition
   (2) government regulation of prices
   (3) inflation
   (4) a growing economy
   (5) a shrinking economy

4. What happens to the price and supply of an item once it is above the equilibrium point on the graph?

   (1) Price goes up; supply goes down.
   (2) Price goes up; supply goes up.
   (3) Price goes down; supply goes down.
   (4) Price goes down; supply goes up.
   (5) Price and supply remain balanced.

5. What is one disadvantage of price regulation?

   One disadvantage of price regulation is

   (1) that costs of items remain affordable
   (2) that demand for items decreases
   (3) that costs of items increase greatly
   (4) that when potential profit is limited, there is less incentive to produce goods
   (5) that when potential profit is limited, there is more incentive to produce goods

UNIT 5

Compare and Contrast Visuals

① Learn the Skill

When you **compare** two or more **visual elements**, you consider the similarities between them. Details about each item are used to gain insight into the other items.

Once you have compared the items, you can **contrast** them. To contrast is to focus only on the differences. As you contrast items, you prepare yourself to analyze why the differences exist.

② Practice the Skill

By mastering the skill of comparing and contrasting, you will improve your study and test-taking skills, especially as they relate to the GED Social Studies Test. Examine the table and map below. Then answer the question that follows.

Ⓐ When analyzing two visuals, look for similarities and differences.

Ⓑ Look for ways to connect the information in order to answer the question. How might changes in income levels affect a family's ability to afford a new home?

EST. MEDIAN NEW HOME PRICE, 2007	
STATE	**MEDIAN NEW HOME PRICE**
Ⓐ New Mexico	Ⓑ $210,000
Idaho	$230,000
Wyoming	$236,000
Montana	$237,000
Utah	$289,000
Oregon	$302,000
Arizona	$317,000
Nevada	$326,000
Washington	$352,000
Colorado	$360,000
California	$519,000

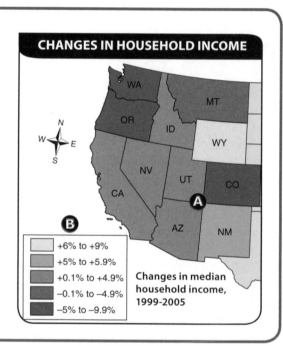

CHANGES IN HOUSEHOLD INCOME

+6% to +9%	
+5% to +5.9%	
+0.1% to +4.9%	Changes in median household income, 1999-2005
−0.1% to −4.9%	
−5% to −9.9%	

☑ TEST-TAKING TIPS

Examine graphics in testing materials thoroughly. Be sure you understand the information shown before trying to answer the questions. You can always assume that two items presented together on the GED Test will have some connection.

1. In which state might residents have the most difficulty in affording a new home?

    (1) California
    (2) Nevada
    (3) New Mexico
    (4) Oregon
    (5) Colorado

③ Apply the Skill

Directions: Choose the <u>one best answer</u> to each question.

<u>Questions 2 through 5</u> refer to the following table and graph.

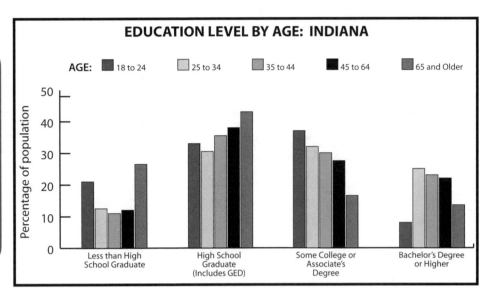

AVERAGE ANNUAL EARNINGS BY EDUCATION: 2006	
EDUCATION LEVEL	**AVG. ANNUAL EARNINGS**
No High School Diploma	$20,873
High School Diploma or GED	$31,071
Bachelor's Degree	$56,788
Advanced Degree	$82,320

2. What can you infer by comparing and contrasting information on the two graphics?

(1) Younger people have the best-paying jobs.
(2) Most people retire at age 65.
(3) People do not need a higher education to be successful.
(4) There is a connection between level of education and degree of economic success.
(5) Success is a matter of luck.

3. Based on the graphics, which of the following is possible?

(1) Twenty-five percent of Indiana residents aged 25 to 34 earn on average more than $56,000 per year.
(2) Most Indiana residents aged 65 and older only make, on average, around $20,000 per year.
(3) Indiana residents aged 18 to 24 have the highest average annual salaries.
(4) Most Indiana residents aged 35 to 44 have a Bachelor's Degree or higher.
(5) Around 35 percent of Indiana residents aged 45 to 64 earn on average $82,320 per year.

4. What cannot be determined by the graphics?

You cannot determine

(1) the average annual earnings for people with GED certificates
(2) which percentage of 30-year-old Hoosiers graduated from high school
(3) the percentage of Indiana residents with an earning potential of more than $82,000 per year
(4) the average annual earnings for 27 percent of Indiana residents aged 65 and older
(5) the earnings limitations for people without a high school diploma or GED certificate

5. Braden, a 20-year-old Indiana resident, has just earned his GED certificate. What is his average annual earnings potential?

(1) around $20,000
(2) around $30,000
(3) around $40,000
(4) around $50,000
(5) around $60,000

UNIT 5

Draw Conclusions from Multiple Sources

① Learn the Skill

In Unit 2, you learned that an **inference** is an educated guess based on available facts and evidence. Later, in Unit 3, you learned that a **conclusion** is a judgment you make by putting together two or more inferences. When learning about social studies, you will often be asked to make inferences and use them to **draw conclusions from multiple sources** of information.

② Practice the Skill

By mastering the skill of drawing conclusions from multiple sources, you will improve your study and test-taking skills, especially as they relate to the GED Social Studies Test. Examine the circle graphs below. Then answer the question that follows.

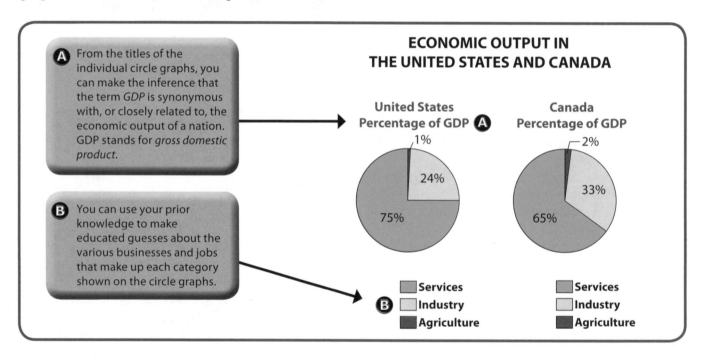

A From the titles of the individual circle graphs, you can make the inference that the term *GDP* is synonymous with, or closely related to, the economic output of a nation. GDP stands for *gross domestic product*.

B You can use your prior knowledge to make educated guesses about the various businesses and jobs that make up each category shown on the circle graphs.

ECONOMIC OUTPUT IN THE UNITED STATES AND CANADA

United States Percentage of GDP **A**
1%
24%
75%

Canada Percentage of GDP
2%
33%
65%

B
Services
Industry
Agriculture

Services
Industry
Agriculture

USING LOGIC

Consider whether the information contained in the sources is similar or different from one another. Also think about whether the information presented in one graph gives you new insight on the information in the other graph.

1. Based on these circle graphs, which of the following conclusions can be drawn?

Based on these graphs, one can conclude that

(1) farming is more important to the economy of the United States than to that of Canada
(2) the United States and Canada have similar economies
(3) Canada has a larger annual GDP than the United States
(4) the United States is more industrialized than Canada
(5) Canada relies more on the service industry than the United States

Directions: Choose the <u>one best answer</u> to each question.

Questions 2 and 3 refer to the following information and graph.

The term *unemployment* refers to the state in which a person who is willing and able to work cannot find a job. For industrial nations, unemployment typically occurs during periods of depression and recession.

U.S. EMPLOYMENT RATE, 1948-2007

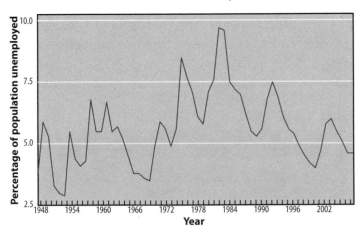

2. Which of the following statements accurately describes unemployment in the United States?

   (1) The nation's unemployment rate has risen steadily since the 1950s.
   (2) The unemployment rate rose to unprecedented levels during the 1980s.
   (3) The rate of employed people in the nation has never dropped to less than 90 percent.
   (4) The nation has experienced alternating periods of rising and falling unemployment over time.
   (5) A spike in the unemployment rate coincided with the beginning of U.S. involvement in the Korean War in 1950.

3. In which period did the United States likely experience its most severe recession of the past 60 years?

   (1) from 1948 to 1954
   (2) from 1966 to 1972
   (3) from 1978 to 1984
   (4) from 1984 to 1990
   (5) from 1996 to 2002

Questions 4 and 5 refer to the following information.

The Dow Jones Industrial Average is a set of indicators that measures changes in the performances of different groupings of stocks. Today, the industrial average includes 30 stocks. The number and selection of stocks have changed over time in order to reflect changes in the U.S. economy. Many people use the Dow Jones Industrial Average as an indicator for both the growth of the stock market and the strength of the economy.

DOW JONES INDUSTRIAL AVERAGE, 1985-2005			
YEAR	DOW AT START OF YEAR	DOW AT CLOSE OF YEAR	CHANGE
1985	1198.87	1546.67	+27.6%
1990	2810.15	2633.66	-4.34%
1995	3838.48	5117.12	+33.45
2000	11357.51	10786.85	-6.18%
2005	10729.43	10717.50	-0.61%

4. Which of the following most likely occurred between 1995 and 2000?

   (1) The U.S. economy grew significantly stronger.
   (2) Unemployment skyrocketed.
   (3) Many new businesses went bankrupt.
   (4) The United States entered a period of recession.
   (5) The prices of stocks remained mostly stable.

5. Why might the year 2000 be seen as a better economic year than 1990?

   (1) The percentage of increase during the year 2000 was higher than that of 1990.
   (2) The year 2000 was a presidential election year.
   (3) The Dow had more stocks listed in 2000 than in 1990.
   (4) Despite a decrease over the course of the year, the Dow started significantly higher in 2000 than 1990.
   (5) The year 2000 was the only year in which the Dow had more than 10,000 points.

Interpret Pictographs

① Learn the Skill

Pictographs are visuals that use symbols to illustrate data in chart form. Pictographs are very versatile because their symbols can represent any type of item. These symbols can also represent any quantity of the featured item. A single symbol could represent one dollar of income or one million members of a population group.

② Practice the Skill

By mastering the skill of interpreting pictographs, you will improve your study and test-taking skills, especially as they relate to the GED Social Studies Test. Examine the pictograph below. Then answer the question that follows.

Ⓐ The key plays a crucial role in your interpretation of a pictograph. It identifies the symbol used in the pictograph, and also gives its value so you can then calculate the values represented on the chart itself.

Ⓑ At times, the symbol will appear in partial or incomplete form. In these instances, the incomplete symbols represent some portion of the full quantity indicated by the full symbol.

**TOP U.S. TRADE PARTNERS:
TOTAL TRADE VALUE OF GOODS, 2007**

Canada

China

Mexico

Japan

Germany **Ⓑ**

United Kingdom

Ⓐ

= $100 billion

Value of trade goods

Country

🧩 MAKING ASSUMPTIONS

You can assume that when interpreting a pictograph, you will be asked to estimate the values represented by the symbols on the chart. Pictographs are not used to identify an exact measure of something, but can show how the value has changed over time, or how it compares to other similar items.

1. What is the total value of goods traded between the United States and Japan?

    The total value of goods traded between the United States and Japan is approximately

    (1) $100 billion
    (2) $150 billion
    (3) $200 billion
    (4) $350 billion
    (5) $550 billion

UNIT 5

Directions: Choose the <u>one best answer</u> to each question.

Questions 2 and 3 refer to the following pictograph.

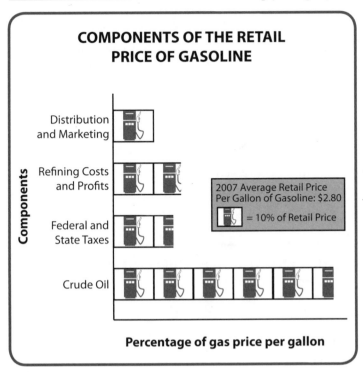

COMPONENTS OF THE RETAIL PRICE OF GASOLINE

2007 Average Retail Price Per Gallon of Gasoline: $2.80
= 10% of Retail Price

Components: Distribution and Marketing, Refining Costs and Profits, Federal and State Taxes, Crude Oil

Percentage of gas price per gallon

Questions 4 and 5 refer to the following pictograph.

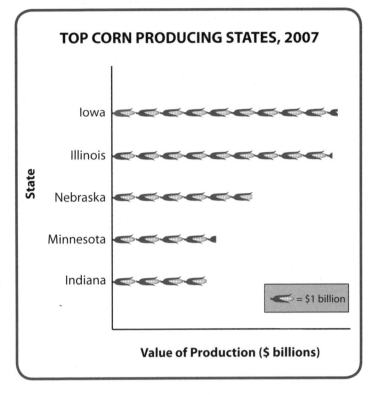

TOP CORN PRODUCING STATES, 2007

State: Iowa, Illinois, Nebraska, Minnesota, Indiana

= $1 billion

Value of Production ($ billions)

2. Approximately what percentage of the cost for an average gallon of gas do federal and state taxes represent?

   (1) 10 percent
   (2) 15 percent
   (3) 25 percent
   (4) 40 percent
   (5) 55 percent

3. Which of the following events would likely have the greatest effect on the cost of a gallon of gasoline?

   The event that would likely have the greatest effect on the cost of a gallon of gasoline would be

   (1) a federal tax increase
   (2) a decrease in rates for television marketing
   (3) severe weather that makes distribution of gasoline more challenging
   (4) a scientific development that reduces the costs of refining
   (5) a decrease in the cost of crude oil

4. Which of the following statements is true based on the information in the pictograph?

   (1) The value of corn production in Iowa exceeded $9 billion.
   (2) Illinois produced about $1 billion worth of corn less than Iowa.
   (3) The value of corn production in Nebraska remained below $5 billion.
   (4) The value of Indiana's corn production was about half that of Illinois.
   (5) Minnesota ranked third in the nation in the value of corn production.

5. What can be inferred from the information in the pictograph?

   (1) Corn is the crop most grown in Illinois.
   (2) Ohio does not produce corn.
   (3) Iowa produces more than twice as much corn as Nebraska.
   (4) The Midwest grows most of the corn produced in the United States.
   (5) The states in the pictograph have few industries.

UNIT 5

Interpret Multi-Bar and Line Graphs

£ ¥ F DM $

① Learn the Skill

When studying economics, you will often encounter data presented in **multi-bar and line graphs**. Like single-bar and line graphs, these visuals can be used to compare values and to show changes over time. However, because they use more than one bar or line, they also allow for the comparison of varied, but connected, data over time

② Practice the Skill

By mastering the skill of interpreting multi-bar and line graphs, you will improve your study and test-taking skills, especially as they relate to the GED Social Studies Test. Examine the double-bar graph below. Then answer the question that follows.

A By studying the bars of a double-bar graph, you can compare two quantities at a given time, as well as the ways in which these quantities change over time.

B The key of a double-bar graph will typically use color or shading to identify what each bar represents. In this graph, one bar represents the average annual mortgage rate, while the other represents the average annual prime interest rate.

AVERAGE ANNUAL MORTGAGE & PRIME INTEREST RATE

B

- Average Annual Mortgage Rate
- Average Annual Prime Interest Rate

Percentage Rate (y-axis: 0, 5, 10, 15, 20)

Year (x-axis: 1980, 1990, 2000)

☑ TEST-TAKING TIPS

When studying a multi-bar or line graph, try to look for patterns among the data shown. Try to determine whether items featured on the graph follow similar or opposite patterns over the period of time shown on the graph. Recognizing these patterns will help you respond to questions more quickly.

1. Based on the double-bar graph above, which of the following statements is true?

(1) In 2000, the average mortgage rate was higher than the average prime interest rate.
(2) The average prime interest rate in 1990 was about 15 percent.
(3) The average mortgage rate in 2000 was about 12 percent.
(4) The average mortgage rate dropped by about 2 percent between 1990 and 2000.
(5) The average prime interest rate increased by about 5 percent between 1980 and 1990.

UNIT 5

Directions: Choose the <u>one best answer</u> to each question.

Questions 2 through 5 refer to the following information and graph.

   The Federal Reserve, or Fed as it is popularly known, is the central bank of both the United States government and the nation's banking system. The Fed regulates banks, in addition to issuing currency and carrying out monetary policy for the nation. One of the Fed's most notable functions is its control of the nation's money supply. To increase the nation's money supply, the Federal Reserve can purchase U.S. Treasury securities from banks and the American public. This will inject new cash into the economy. The Fed can also increase the money supply by lowering the discount rate, or the interest rate at which it lends to commercial banks. This will encourage banks to borrow more money from the Fed, thereby raising the money supply. In the United States, money supply is evaluated in four different categories, or measures. Items are placed into these categories according to their liquidity, or how easily they can be turned into cash. The first category, M1, features cash, traveler's checks, and checking accounts from which deposits can be made on demand. The second category, M2, includes all of M1, plus savings deposits worth less than $100,000.

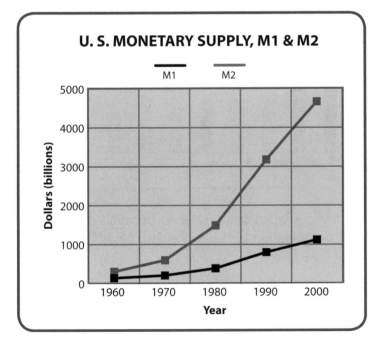

2. Which of the following statements will always be true?

   (1) The value of M1 exceeds $150 billion.
   (2) The value of M2 is increasing steadily.
   (3) The value of M2 is greater than that of M1.
   (4) The value of M1 is approximately one-half the value of M2.
   (5) The value of M2 does not exceed $5,000 billion.

3. What was the approximate value of M1 in 1970?

   The value of M1 in 1970 was approximately

   (1) $200 billion
   (2) $800 billion
   (3) $1000 billion
   (4) $1800 billion
   (5) $2300 billion

4. In which year was the value of M2 over M1 the greatest?

   (1) 1960
   (2) 1970
   (3) 1980
   (4) 1990
   (5) 2000

5. Based on the information, in which year did the economy probably have the most liquidity?

   The year with the most liquidity was probably

   (1) 1960
   (2) 1970
   (3) 1980
   (4) 1990
   (5) 2000

Predict Outcomes

① Learn the Skill

Often in the study of economics, you will want to make a **prediction**, or a suggestion about what might happen next, after drawing conclusions. To **predict outcomes**, you must access your prior knowledge and experiences about a subject. Then, by applying this information to existing patterns that you recognize, you can make a prediction.

② Practice the Skill

By mastering the skill of predicting outcomes, you will improve your study and test-taking skills, especially as they relate to the GED Social Studies Test. Examine the bar graphs below. Then answer the question that follows.

A Consider how supply and demand might influence where a company decides to look for new employees. Companies want to have a large supply of qualified candidates, but also need to keep salary costs down in order to increase profits.

B Together, these graphs reveal a pattern that can help you answer the question. Identify the nation that ranks high in the ratio of engineering degrees to bachelor degrees, yet low in annual salary.

🧩 MAKING ASSUMPTIONS

For the purposes of answering this question, you can assume that the company in question is motivated solely by the desire to make a profit. In reality, companies may consider other factors, such as government policies or public opinion, before deciding to outsource jobs to another country.

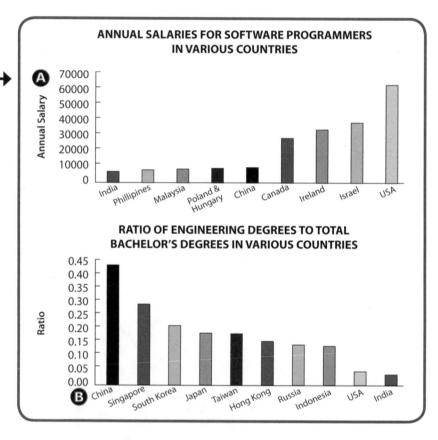

ANNUAL SALARIES FOR SOFTWARE PROGRAMMERS IN VARIOUS COUNTRIES

RATIO OF ENGINEERING DEGREES TO TOTAL BACHELOR'S DEGREES IN VARIOUS COUNTRIES

1. Where would you predict that a U.S. corporation could find the best combination of highly trained, yet affordable prospective engineers?

    (1) United States
    (2) Israel
    (3) China
    (4) Russia
    (5) Ireland

UNIT 5

Directions: Choose the <u>one best answer</u> to each question.

<u>Questions 2 and 3</u> refer to the following information and bar graph.

Telecommuting is a system in which employees work from home, or some other location, instead of at an employer's office. These employees maintain close communication with their employers through the use of telephones, e-mail, and fax machines. As technology improved during the 1990s, telecommuting became increasingly popular in the United States. By 1999, approximately 10 million U.S. workers regularly telecommuted. Proponents of telecommuting argue that it increases productivity, saves gasoline, and decreases pollution and congestion caused by traffic. Telecommuting can also allow companies to retain highly regarded employees who are unable or unwilling to work in the office. On the other hand, critics suggest that telecommuting can make it difficult for managerial workers to supervise their telecommuting employees.

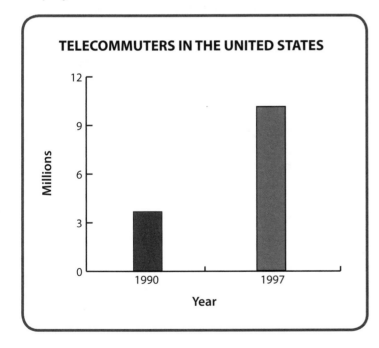

2. Which of the following tasks would be the most difficult for a telecommuting employee?

   (1) reading company announcements
   (2) sending and receiving e-mail
   (3) participating in team building exercises
   (4) maintaining schedules and deadlines
   (5) taking part in company conference calls

3. Consider the ways in which technology in the United States has changed since 1997.

   Based on your prior knowledge and the pattern shown in this graph, which of the following predictions would you make?

   (1) The number of telecommuters held steady for several years after 1997.
   (2) The number of telecommuters returned to its 1990 level.
   (3) The number of telecommuters decreased gradually in the years after 1997.
   (4) The number of telecommuters continued to increase steadily in the years after 1997.
   (5) The number of telecommuters decreased sharply in the years after 1997.

<u>Question 4</u> refers to the following information.

In November 2008, leaders of the "Big Three" automakers (Ford, Chrysler, General Motors) asked members of the U.S. House and Senate for billions of dollars in loans or a financial bailout.

4. Assume that the legislature did not provide the money. What might be a potential outcome from that decision?

   (1) Stimulus checks will not be sent to American taxpayers.
   (2) Taxes will increase.
   (3) Many U.S. banks will fail.
   (4) There will be a negative impact on international trade.
   (5) The mayor of Detroit will be impeached.

Unit 5 Review

The Unit Review is structured to resemble the GED Social Studies Test. Be sure to read each question and all possible answers very carefully before choosing your answer.

To record your answers, fill in the numbered circle that corresponds to the answer you select for each question in the Unit Review.

Do not rest your pencil on the answer area while considering your answer. Make no stray or unnecessary marks. If you change an answer, erase your first mark completely.

Mark only one answer space for each question; multiple answers will be scored as incorrect.

Sample Question

Why might capitalist governments regulate businesses?

(1) to protect the safety of workers
(2) to control the prices of goods
(3) to direct the companies to make certain products
(4) to force the companies to hire only male workers
(5) to enhance the overall economy of the government

●②③④⑤

Directions: Choose the one best answer to each question.

Questions 1 through 3 refer to the following information.

A mixed economy is an economic system that operates partially as a free market capitalist economy. However, other parts of a mixed economy are operated by the government, as in a Socialist economy.

India represents one notable example of a mixed economy. From the time of the nation's independence from Britain, the Indian government worked to control industry in the nation. Beginning in the late 1970s, the government slowly began to relinquish control of some elements of the economy. However, by 1991 the state still controlled important parts of India's economy, including the mining, banking, transportation, communications, and manufacturing industries.

Following a major financial crisis in 1991, the Indian government began to pursue more effective economic reforms. The goals of these reforms included deregulating industries and privatizing public sector industries such as aviation, power, and telecommunications. Today, some industries remain under government control. These include India's nuclear power, defense, and railway industries.

1. Which of the following caused India to institute significant economic reforms?

(1) independence from Britain
(2) the deregulation of the nation's industries
(3) a major economic crisis
(4) the growth of the nation's banking industry
(5) the privatization of India's public sector

①②③④⑤

2. Which U.S. sector has a similar level of government control as India's railway industry?

(1) public primary and secondary education
(2) manufacturing
(3) transportation
(4) communications
(5) defense equipment

①②③④⑤

3. Which part of India's economy represents socialism?

(1) the power industry
(2) telecommunications
(3) nuclear power
(4) aviation
(5) agriculture

①②③④⑤

Questions 4 through 6 refer to the following pictograph.

U.S. OUTSTANDING NATIONAL DEBT, 1960-2005

4. Which of the following actions would guarantee a reduction in the level of the U.S. national debt?

   (1) a lengthy term in office for a president from one political party
   (2) the approval of a federal budget that produces a surplus dedicated to paying money owed to other nations
   (3) the discontinuation of many government programs
   (4) an increase in tax benefits given to large corporations
   (5) the passage of new legislation to stimulate economic growth in the nation
   ①②③④⑤

5. Which of the following statements can you determine to be true based on the pictograph?

   (1) The U.S. national debt had exceeded $400 billion by 1970.
   (2) The U.S. national debt decreased between 1980 and 1985.
   (3) The U.S. national debt expanded more between 1995 and 2000 than it did between 2000 and 2005.
   (4) The national debt level has continued to rise since 1970.
   (5) The United States did not spend more money than it received prior to 1960.
   ①②③④⑤

6. What was the approximate value of the U.S. national debt in 1995?

   (1) $500 billion
   (2) $750 billion
   (3) $2.5 trillion
   (4) $4.7 trillion
   (5) $7 trillion
   ①②③④⑤

Question 7 refers to the following information.

For Federal agencies, telework is of particular interest for its benefits in the following areas:
   • Recruiting and retaining the best possible workforce …
   • Helping employees manage long commutes and other work/life issues that, if not addressed, can have a negative impact on their effectiveness or lead to employees leaving Federal employment
   • Reducing traffic congestion, emissions, and infrastructure impact in urban areas, thereby improving the environment
   • Saving taxpayer dollars by decreasing Government real estate costs
   • Ensuring continuity of essential Government functions in the event of national or local emergencies

From *A Guide to Telework in the Federal Government*

7. Which of the following predictions can you make based on this excerpt?

   (1) The amount of telework in the federal government will decrease over time.
   (2) Telework will make government work less efficient.
   (3) Government work will be completed more affordably through further implementation of telework.
   (4) Telework can benefit all federal employees.
   (5) Automobile manufacturers would strongly support the implementation of federal telework programs.
   ①②③④⑤

UNIT 5

Questions 8 through 10 refer to the following information.

An economic depression is a crisis period in which unemployment rises, prices drop, and credit is restricted. These periods are further characterized by reduced economic investment and output, as well as large numbers of bankruptcies.

Depressions usually begin through a combination of decreases in demand and overproduction. These factors lead to decreased production, workforce reductions, and diminished wages for employees. As these changes weaken consumers' purchasing power, a depression can worsen and become more widespread. Recovery from a depression typically requires either the existing overstock of goods to be depleted or the emergence of new markets. At times, government intervention may be necessary to stimulate an economic recovery. Due to today's global economy, present-day depressions often spread around the world.

REAL U.S. GROSS DOMESTIC PRODUCT, 1929-1939 (2000 DOLLARS)	
YEAR	REAL GDP (BILLIONS IN VALUE OF 2000 DOLLARS)
1929	865.2
1930	790.7
1931	739.9
1932	643.7
1933	635.5
1934	704.2
1935	766.9
1936	866.6
1937	911.1
1938	879.7
1939	950.7

8. Which of the following conclusions can be drawn based on the information?

It can be concluded that

(1) the United States had been in a period of recession throughout the 1920s
(2) the production of war supplies for World War II led to a depression in the United States
(3) the purchasing power of U.S. consumers grew increasingly weak during the early 1930s.
(4) the United States had fully recovered from a depression by 1934
(5) government intervention in the U.S. economy proved unnecessary during the 1930s

① ② ③ ④ ⑤

9. Which of the following predictions could you make about the years following 1939?

(1) The United States would experience a growing number of bankruptcies.
(2) The GDP of the United States would rise and fall repeatedly.
(3) Decreases in demand would continue to drive prices down.
(4) Depression conditions would become more severe throughout the nation.
(5) Unemployment in the United States would gradually decrease.

① ② ③ ④ ⑤

10. Why does the table show the U.S. GDP in year 2000 dollars?

(1) inflation
(2) overproduction
(3) unemployment
(4) supply and demand
(5) changes in business confidence

① ② ③ ④ ⑤

Questions 11 through 14 refer to the following information and flowchart.

Factors of production are the items used to complete a production process. These factors typically fall into three main categories—land, labor, and capital. At times, a fourth category, defined as entrepreneurship or management, also appears alongside these. In order for a business to achieve success, it must maintain a healthy balance of these factors of production.

The flowchart below shows the flow of money, as well as goods and services, throughout the U.S. economy. In this flowchart, households own all of the factors of production. The people in these households sell their labor, land, and capital to firms. In exchange for these factors of production, the people receive wages, rent, and profits.

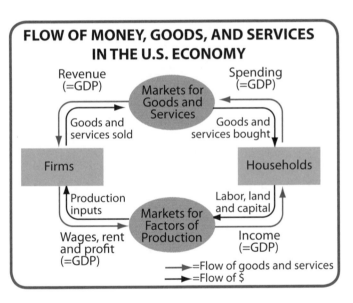

11. Suppose you own a company that manufactures lawnmowers.

Which of the following factors of production would fall under the category of labor?

(1) money contributed by shareholders in your company
(2) your ideas and innovations for new products
(3) the property on which your company is located
(4) the work of your employees
(5) your ability to effectively manage your employees

①②③④⑤

12. Which type of factor of production is your willingness to start your own business and manufacture products?

The willingness to start one's own business and manufacture products is an example of

(1) land
(2) labor
(3) capital
(4) profit
(5) entrepreneurship

①②③④⑤

13. Which of the following actions generates revenue for firms?

(1) buying goods and services from people in households
(2) selling goods and services to people in households
(3) buying factors of production from households
(4) selling factors of production to households
(5) avoiding the markets for goods and services and factors of production

①②③④⑤

14. Based on the information and flowchart, which of the following statements can you determine to be true?

(1) Firms control all of the production inputs in this economic system.
(2) All transactions between firms and households contribute to the nation's GDP.
(3) Households generate income by selling goods and services.
(4) After receiving wages, rent, and profit, firms use these items to purchase factors of production.
(5) Money and goods and services move in the same direction throughout this economic system.

①②③④⑤

Questions 15 through 18 refer to the following graphs.

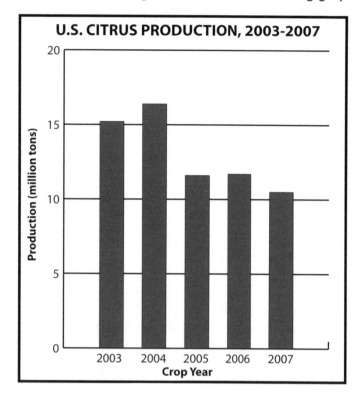

U.S. CITRUS PRODUCTION, 2003-2007

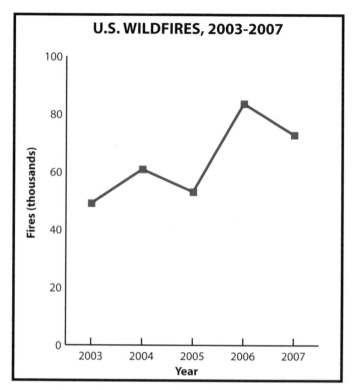

U.S. WILDFIRES, 2003-2007

15. On both graphs, examine the changes that took place between 2005 and 2007.

These changes could be multiple effects of which common cause?

(1) an increased budget for forestry agencies
(2) cool, damp conditions in the western United States
(3) a nationwide drought
(4) efforts to increase demand for agricultural products
(5) increased efforts to reduce the effects of natural disasters

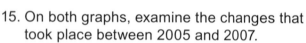

16. The common cause shared by these changes could have also produced which of the following effects?

This cause could have also produced

(1) higher vegetable prices
(2) decreased citrus imports
(3) increased habitat for wildlife
(4) employment of fewer emergency personnel
(5) flooding in many parts of the nation

①②③④⑤

17. In which year shown on the graph did the U.S. citrus production peak?

U.S. citrus production peaked in

(1) 2003
(2) 2004
(3) 2005
(4) 2006
(5) 2007

①②③④⑤

18. Between which periods did the number of U.S. wildfires increase the most?

U.S. wildfires increased the most between

(1) 2002 and 2003
(2) 2003 and 2004
(3) 2004 and 2005
(4) 2005 and 2006
(5) 2006 and 2007

①②③④⑤

UNIT 5

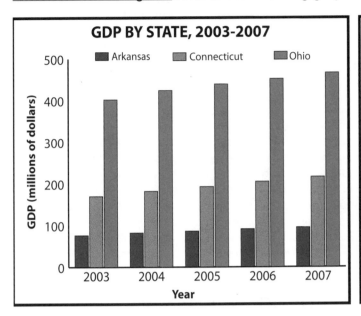

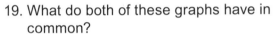

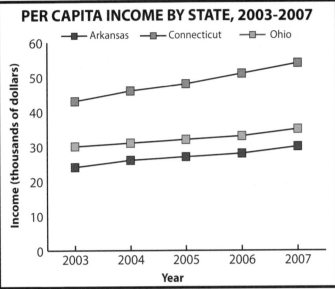

19. What do both of these graphs have in common?

Both of the graphs

(1) highlight the need for manufacturing growth in the United States
(2) demonstrate the effects of inflation
(3) provide information about the economic status of individual states
(4) show the effects of unemployment on state economies
(5) span a ten-year period of time

①②③④⑤

20. Which of the following statements can you determine to be true based on these graphs?

(1) The GDP and per capita income of Arkansas remained at about 50 percent of those of Ohio for the period shown.
(2) For each state, the GDP and per capita income increased at similar rates.
(3) The period from 2007 to 2011 would likely feature steady increases in GDP and per capita income for each state.
(4) The GDP and per capita income of Ohio grew at a slower rate than those of Arkansas and Connecticut.
(5) GDP and per capita income are not related.

①②③④⑤

21. Which of the following can you conclude based on these graphs?

(1) Imports to Ohio have decreased each year since 2003.
(2) The most important industries in Connecticut and Arkansas are highly similar.
(3) The GDP of Arkansas and Connecticut will eventually reach the same level.
(4) Connecticut has a smaller population than Ohio.
(5) The population of Arkansas is expanding at a higher rate than that at which its wages are increasing.

①②③④⑤

22. Unlike the multi-line graph, the multi-bar graph does not take into account which of the following items when measuring the data?

(1) the history of each state
(2) the national standard for its subject
(3) the variety of industries found in each state
(4) the number of businesses located in each state
(5) the population of each state ("per capita")

①②③④⑤

UNIT 5

Answer Key

UNIT 1 GEOGRAPHY

LESSON 1, *pp. 2–3*
1. Analysis: (1), Brazil is in South America and is the only choice that is on the equator.
2. Analysis: (3), Ecuador's climate is different in the mountains, along the coast, and in the Amazon.
3. Comprehension: (4), People moved to the Costa region because of increased banana production.
4. Application: (5), The Sierra region features the Andes Mountains.

LESSON 2, *pp. 4–5*
1. Comprehension: (4), There are five major cities in northeastern New Jersey, more than in any other area.
2. Application: (4), Sydney is the only city east of 150˚E longitude.
3. Analysis: (1), Looking at the map, it is easy to see that most of the cities are located along the coast.
4. Comprehension: (2), The star symbol indicates that Atlanta is the capital. Interstate 75 goes through Atlanta.
5. Comprehension: (5), Highways 280 and 16 merge in Savannah.
6. Application: (5), Savannah is the closest city to those coordinates.

LESSON 3, *pp. 6–7*
1. Evaluation: (1), The shading on the map indicates that the elevation of California is varied and has low land, hills, and mountains.
2. Application: (4), There are five Great Lakes and Michigan borders four of them.
3. Evaluation: (4), Silver Lake State Park is on the east coast of Lake Michigan.
4. Comprehension: (3), The coastal areas receive more than 60 inches of rain a year, making them the wettest areas.
5. Analysis: (3), The shading on the map indicates that the lowest amount of precipitation along the Florida border is between 52 and 56 inches.

LESSON 4, *pp. 8–9*
1. Comprehension: (3), This map shows the counties in Wyoming and Wyoming's bordering states.
2. Analysis: (5), The shading on the map indicates that most of the population density is located near the major cities.
3. Application: (1), Madrid has the largest area with more than 965 people per square mile.
4. Application: (2), The most logical option is that Tucson is both a large city and the county seat.
5. Application: (1), Even though Coconino County has a larger area, most of the large cities are in Maricopa County. Therefore, it can be assumed that Maricopa County has the largest population.

LESSON 5, *pp. 10–11*
1. Analysis: (4), After the founding of Jamestown, slave traders began taking slaves to North America.
2. Analysis: (5), It is logical to assume that both trade goods and ideas were exchanged among countries along the Silk Road.
3. Application: (2), The best route from Alexandria to Kabul is through Seleucia and Bactra.

LESSON 6, *pp. 12–13*
1. Evaluation: (2), Caring for refugees was expensive, so if Tanzania had a large refugee population, then they affected Tanzania's economy.
2. Analysis: (4), The Confederacy launched an attack over open ground. Their troops were stretched thin, while the Union had a more compact battle line.
3. Analysis: (1), Austria-Hungary and Serbia no longer existed in 1919 (after World War I). Their lands were divided into several new countries.

UNIT 1 REVIEW, *pp. 14–19*
1. Analysis: (2), This general description best explains Beijing's relative location.
2. Application: (5), Latitude and longitude are used to find absolute location.
3. Evaluation: (5), All of the states that border the Gulf of Mexico are in the southern region.
4. Analysis: (2), Nashville is in Tennessee. It is the only answer choice in a southern region state.
5. Application: (3), Using the scale, you can measure the distance at around 700 miles.
6. Comprehension: (4), The majority of the population lives in the southeast, near Ottawa.
7. Application: (5), Because Alberta has the highest population of the provinces listed, it most likely has the highest total income.
8. Analysis: (2), Because the majority of the population lives along or near the Atlantic coast or the Great Lakes, you can logically assume that fishing and shipping are important industries.
9. Comprehension: (1), Follow the lines of latitude and longitude to determine that Yellowknife is the closest city to those coordinates.
10. Application: (5), The routes on the map show that African Americans from Georgia most likely migrated to an east coast state such as New York.
11. Analysis: (3), World War I was happening in Europe in 1916. This led to an increase in manufacturing jobs. Jim Crow laws promoted discrimination in the South. These two factors most contributed to the Great Migration.
12. Analysis: (4), The Harlem Renaissance was a result of the migration of African American artists, authors, and musicians to New York during this period.
13. Application: (1), The United States saw an increase in its urban (city) workforce during the Great Migration.
14. Comprehension: (2), Of the states listed, Nevada has the lowest annual rate of precipitation.

UNIT 1 (continued)

15. Application: (3), The Pacific coast area has the greatest diversity in precipitation levels so logically it has the most diverse climate.

16. Application: (1), The map shows that the French had more troops and cannons.

17. Application: (2), With their back against the Alle River, the Russians became trapped as the French advanced.

18. Comprehension: (4), All of the early settlements were built along waterways.

19. Analysis: (1), The American Revolution ended in 1783. The settlements on the map were all founded soon after that date.

UNIT 2 U.S. HISTORY

LESSON 1, pp. 22–23

1. Comprehension: (2), Using the columns and rows in the table, you can determine that the New England colonies included Connecticut and New Hampshire.

2. Comprehension: (2), The data in the table supports only the fact that New York had a larger population than Delaware. Rhode Island is the smallest state, but in 1750, it did not have the smallest population. Pennsylvania had the fourth largest population, but that did not mean that it was the fourth largest colony in terms of geographic area.

3. Analysis: (4), This question requires you to use both logic and your knowledge of history. The smallest colonies did not have the smallest populations (Georgia and Connecticut disprove this). Neither Massachusetts (second largest population) nor Maryland (third largest population) were Southern Colonies. Both the New England and Middle Colonies had more than one populous colony. The populations of both New York and Georgia would increase dramatically after 1750. The only correct choice is that the earliest colonies (Virginia, Massachusetts, Pennsylvania, and Maryland) had larger populations that colonies established closer to 1750 (Georgia). This is also the logical choice. If a colony was founded shortly before 1750, its population would logically be much smaller than colonies established in the 1600s.

4. Application: (5), The data on the table clearly shows that the population of Virginia increased dramatically between 1700 and 1750. Therefore, you need to find the answer choice that would logically and reasonably support this trend. The first three choices would indicate a decrease in population not an increase. Choice 4 is not logical. Choice 5 is correct. A diversified agricultural economy is a positive change and would encourage more people to move to Virginia because they would be able to support themselves and make a profit.

LESSON 2, pp. 24–25

1. Comprehension: (3), In his pamphlet, Thomas Paine clearly states that the bravest achievements are accomplished by young nations.

2. Analysis: (3), The challenge here is to identify the main idea. Most answer choices include details from the Declaration of Independence, but only choice 3 clearly explains the main idea that people have the right to end destructive governments and form new ones. Details such as unalienable rights support this main idea.

3. Analysis: (4), The correct answer is that the colonists cautiously approached independence only after the British continued to violently oppress them. This is clear through the details in the paragraph. The fact that the Declaration of Independence was written over a year after war broke out between Britain and the colonies is a detail that supports this main idea. Despite having to fight the British army, the colonists' first option was not declaring independence.

4. Application: (1), Because Pennsylvania and Virginia had the largest number of signers of the Declaration of Independence, it is logical to assume that they were large and important colonies.

LESSON 3, pp. 26–27

1. Comprehension: (4), The Anti-Federalists believed that the government should favor agriculture over commerce and industry. Therefore, you can categorize "the future of the nation depends upon the work of farmers throughout the nation" as expressing an Anti-Federalist viewpoint.

2. Analysis: (2), John Jay categorizes those who want America united under a strong government and those who want states to have more power. Therefore, the correct answer is 2: people who believe in a strong central government and people who believe in a number of strong state governments.

3. Evaluation: (5), The Anti-Federalist sentiment in the second excerpt categorizes citizens as people who want a limited government. This is referenced throughout the excerpt, and clearly stated in the last sentence.

4. Analysis: (3), Since this dispute occurred between Georgia and Spain, it is best categorized at international political history.

5. Application: (1), Because Georgia allowed slavery, it is logical to assume that Alabama and Mississippi could be categorized as slave states. New territories within the United States are not colonies, and the question specifically asks about the future states of Alabama and Mississippi (so the answer is not Southern or Spanish colonies).

LESSON 4, pp. 28–29

1. Comprehension: (3), The information states "After taking office in 1829, Jackson spurred Congress to pass the Indian Removal Act of 1830." Therefore, the correct answer is 3.

2. Comprehension: (4), The Battle of Tippecanoe took place in 1811, so it preceded the War of 1812.

UNIT 2 *(continued)*

3. Application: (5), This question requires you to make an assumption. Choice 1 is not reasonable; choice 2 is not true (the United States never controlled Canada); choice 3 is not true (while the Battle of New Orleans did take place after the Treaty of Ghent was signed, Andrew Jackson defeated the British); choice 4 is not logical (the United States was less than 30 years old – it is not logical that the U.S. was the most powerful nation in the world). The correct assumption is choice 5: After defeating the British in the War of 1812, nationalism, or national pride, began to grow in the United States.

4. Comprehension: (3), Texas gained its independence in 1821. The Texas Revolution was in 1835, which was more than 10 years after Texas gained its independence.

LESSON 5, *pp. 30–31*
1. Comprehension: (4), The information states that the Northern economy featured commercial and industrial sectors as well as agriculture. Therefore, one effect of sectional differences between the North and the South was that the Northern economy became increasingly diverse.

2. Evaluation: (3), The table shows that the population of enslaved African Americans in South Carolina grew dramatically over the years. Most enslaved people worked on farms or plantations, especially in South Carolina. Therefore, the most likely cause of the population increase was that agriculture remained the most common way of making a living in the South.

3. Application: (2), This question requires you to use logic. By examining the table, you can clearly see that over time, the growth of the enslaved African American population in South Carolina outpaced that of whites. The most logical effect of this large difference was that whites would become increasingly nervous about possible violence from the enslaved African American population. As a consequence, South Carolina had some of the harshest laws for slaves.

4. Analysis: (5), The last sentence in the paragraph tells you that Turner and his followers received harsh punishments for leading the revolt. It is logical to believe that whites would be afraid of similar action, so Turner's revolt most likely caused southern officials to develop more restrictive policies towards enslaved people.

5. Analysis: (1), The most likely cause of Turner's actions was his (and others) anger over the harsh conditions under which they lived.

LESSON 6, *pp. 32–33*
1. Evaluation: (2), In this case, you should contrast (or find differences) between Lincoln's plan and that of the radical Republicans. Their plans featured different objectives for the process of Reconstruction.

2. Analysis: (3), Although they went about it in different ways, both Lincoln and the radical Republicans wanted to successfully rebuild the United States.

3. Analysis: (1), Compared to the plans of the radical Republicans, Lincoln's Reconstruction plans can be described as peace-making.

4. Analysis: (5), This question requires you to make an assumption. If Sherman set out to demoralize the South, Lee's actions were kind. Therefore, it is logical to assume that Lee believed that by being kind to Northerners the Confederacy might win their support.

5. Application: (4), The ultimate goal for both Sherman and Lee was to find a way to win the war.

LESSON 7, *pp. 34–35*
1. Comprehension: (4), By interpreting the line graph, you can see that the number of manufacturing establishments in Illinois increased from 20,000 to almost 40,000 in the 1890s. This, compared to the growth between 1880 and 1890, was a dramatic increase.

2. Analysis: (4), By analyzing the bar graph, you can determine that the only correct statement is that Taft received nearly 3.5 million popular votes.

3. Evaluation: (1), It is clear by the number of candidates that the 1912 presidential election was a multi-party race.

4. Analysis: (2), This question requires you to use logic and make an assumption. Germany is in western Europe. Russia is in eastern Europe. There were more than 3 million immigrants from western Europe and only about a half-million immigrants from eastern Europe. Therefore, it is logical to assume that in 1890, it is likely that more immigrants to the United States came from Germany than from Russia.

5. Application: (3), The most dramatic statistic in the second circle graph is the number of Irish immigrants to the United States. The likely reason for the large amount of Irish leaving their homeland was the continued eviction of poor Irish farmers.

LESSON 8, *pp. 36–37*
1. Analysis: (2), Because Wilson ran with the campaign slogan "He kept us out of war" and won, it is logical to infer that many Americans supported Wilson's policy of neutrality.

2. Analysis: (3), Because she served as a leader in the National Woman Suffrage Association, the most reasonable inference is that Susan B. Anthony traveled and lectured on the importance of women's suffrage.

3. Analysis: (5), By analyzing the arguments of the authors of *The Blue Book*, you can infer that they believed in using a logical, methodical approach to win an argument.

LESSON 9, *pp. 38–39*
1. Analysis: (2), The text in the cartoon indicates that the cartoonist has disdain for politicians. The character cutting down the tree appears to be a "strong man of the people." Therefore, you can assume that the cartoonist believes that the Prohibition Party is right in trying to outlaw alcohol.

2. Analysis: (2), The lines tying the hands of Uncle Sam (the United States) read "The League of Nations." This indicates that those pulling on the lines are trying to make the United States take their side, meaning that they are competing for their own best interests in the League of Nations.

UNIT 2 (continued)

3. Evaluation: (4), The cartoon suggests that the United States had its hands tied by other groups in the League of Nations. Therefore, it is logical to assume that those parties have prevented the United States from taking any action of its own regarding the League of Nations.

4. Evaluation: (2), Because Hoover is posting a detour sign to indicate the flow away from "Speculation Street" and onto "Business Boulevard," the cartoonist suggests that Hoover is guiding the country's economy back to stability.

LESSON 10, *pp. 40–41*

1. Application: (3), Remember that a short summary does not include specific details. The best summary of the information is that the United States and the Soviet Union competed in a space race for scientific and political gains.

2. Analysis: (5), A summary is an overview, so a summary would likely include an overview of McCarthy's accusations and his eventual downfall.

3. Application: (4), The best summaries include all relevant information but do not offer opinions. Therefore, the best summary of the information is that McCarthy gained power through his hearings on Communism, but then lost it with a series of unfounded accusations.

4. Application: (3), This question is difficult, because here the map is irrelevant. The only correct summary of the information presented is that President Truman authorized various types of U.S. troops to aid South Korean forces.

UNIT 2 REVIEW, *pp. 42–47*

1. Comprehension: (4), Choice 4 is the only one that includes details about how the woman suffrage movement would have been divided.

2. Comprehension: (2), By examining the information in the second column of the table, you can determine that Lyndon B. Johnson was president between 1963 and 1969.

3. Evaluation: (4), Massachusetts, Texas, New York, Illinois, and California all have large populations. Only two of the ten presidents since 1961 have been from less populous states (Georgia and Arkansas). Therefore, most presidents since 1960 have represented states with large populations.

4. Analysis: (1), Remember that the main idea is the entire point of the map, not a detail. All of the details on the map support the main idea that settlers followed several different trails to reach the western United States.

5. Analysis: (5), The only choice that illustrates a danger that may have occurred along the Oregon Trail is that many settlers along the trail died from diseases such as cholera.

6. Comprehension: (4), Use both the *x* and *y* axes to determine that the population of Michigan in 1940 was approximately 5.25 million.

7. Comprehension: (5), The population of Michigan grew by almost 2 million people between 1950 and 1960. Michigan experienced the greatest population growth in that decade.

8. Evaluation: (3), This question requires you to make an assumption. Detroit, Michigan, was and is an important city to the automotive industry. The automotive industry grew dramatically between 1940 and 1960. During that time, Michigan experienced some of its largest population increases. Therefore, you can assume that Michigan's population was affected by the automotive industry.

9. Application: (4), Because one of the Anti-Federalists' main concerns with the original Constitution was that it lacked protection for individual rights, and James Monroe was an Anti-Federalist, it is logical to assume that Monroe supported the Virginia Declaration of Rights, which was the model for the U.S. Constitution's Bill of Rights. The fact that Madison also supported states' rights is also a clue that he probably supported the Virginia Declaration of Rights.

10. Evaluation: (1), The information states that the Federalists favored industries and big business. Therefore, the correct choice is that the Federalists believed that support for industry and trade should come before support of small farmers.

11. Analysis: (2), By analyzing both Lincoln's and Douglas's arguments, you can determine that neither intended to interfere with slavery where it already existed.

12. Evaluation: (4), Be sure to read the question carefully. You are being asked to decide with which of Douglas's assertions Lincoln would disagree. Lincoln clearly believes that all men have natural rights and does not think that states should be able to restrict those rights. Therefore, he would disagree with Douglas's assertion that each state has sovereign power.

13. Analysis: (3), Lyndon B. Johnson's policy was called the Great Society, so the figure on the left in this cartoon is Johnson. Lyndon Johnson is the only answer choice who was a Vietnam era president. The face of the man with the sword is a caricature of Johnson, with a large nose and ears.

14. Analysis: (5), In the cartoon, Johnson beheads a figure representing the Great Society with a sword called War Costs. This violent action illustrates that the costs of taking part in the Vietnam War would take away vital money from the Great Society programs. The action of the sword is more dramatic than accidental neglect.

15. Analysis: (3), The ultimate cause of the Missouri Compromise was fear of the spread of slavery. While it was important to some members of congress to have a balance, the balance needed to have been between free and slave states, not Northern and Southern states.

16. Analysis: (1), Since the information states that the Missouri Compromise preserved the balance of free and slave states in the nation, and each state has two U.S. Senators, then the fact that representation in the Senate would remain equal for free and slave states is an implied effect.

17. Analysis: (2), The first paragraph states that Bush's early foreign policy was dominated by the terrorist attacks on September 11, 2001. The document explaining the purpose of the Department of Homeland Security was dated June 2002. The details about the Department of Homeland Security in the document make it possible to infer that it was created in response to the terrorist attacks.

18. Comprehension: (4), The only choice listed on the sequence chart as having happened before 1867 is that the Union Pacific crews reach the 100th Meridian line, which took place in October 1866.

19. Comprehension: (5), The sequence chart indicates that the first event was the passing of the Pacific Railroad Bill.

20. Application: (1), This question requires that you make an assumption. It is logical to assume that since the railroad would bring both people and goods to new areas, significant economic growth would occur along the railroad lines.

UNIT 3 WORLD HISTORY

LESSON 1, *pp. 50–51*

1. Comprehension: (2), The second paragraph in the information states that Athens established a democracy in which every freeborn man older than 18 received an equal vote. The situation described in the question is also a democracy.

2. Analysis: (5), The first paragraph states that Ancient Egypt was an agrarian society. Agrarian is another word for agriculture. Both paragraphs discuss daily life. Therefore, the concepts which are most important in the text are agriculture and daily life.

3. Analysis: (3), While women in Ancient Egypt did all of the things listed as answer choices, the best way to categorize women in Ancient Egypt is to say that they had many rights.

4. Evaluation: (2), By examining the map, you can see that Athens had control of several places all along the Aegean Sea. As you know, in ancient times, travel by water was faster than travel over land. The information also mentions that both Athens and Sparta had sea trade routes. Combine all of this information to categorize Athens as a naval power.

5. Evaluation: (4), Because both Athens and Sparta were Greek city-states, a conflict between the two, such as the Peloponnesian War, would be considered a civil war. Remember that the American Civil War was fought between two groups of American states.

LESSON 2, *pp. 52–53*

1. Comprehension: (5), When examining a Venn diagram, such as the one on this page, be sure to note what each section of the diagram describes. In this diagram, you need to identify something that France did but England did not. Unlike England, France claimed new territories for the nation.

2. Evaluation: (4), The diagram shows that flying buttresses were used in Gothic architecture, not in Romanesque architecture.

3. Analysis: (4), The diagram shows that Gothic architecture featured pointed arches instead of round. This gave Gothic structures a soaring look. The information also states that Gothic buildings were taller than Romanesque buildings. Therefore, Gothic churches were taller and appeared to be soaring.

4. Application: (3), According to the diagram, medieval tournaments featured jousts on horseback and hand-to-hand melees. Therefore, medieval tournaments were similar to present-day sporting events.

5. Analysis: (5), While knights may have participated in tournaments, the diagram classifies knights as being members of the Court.

LESSON 3, *pp. 54–55*

1. Comprehension: (2), While the text of the *Magna Carta* does discuss the church and archbishops, the main purpose of the document was to establish basic rights of Englishmen.

2. Analysis: (3), In the first paragraph, Locke states that men are in "a state of perfect freedom." Therefore, you can infer that his point of view is that people are naturally free.

3. Analysis: (5), In the second paragraph, Locke states that "unless the lord and master of them all [meaning God] should, by any manifest declaration of his will, set one above another, and confer on him, by an evident and clear appointment, an undoubted right to dominion and sovereignty." He therefore believes that government should promote equality and only be led by a divinely-appointed sovereign.

4. Application: (3), Thomas Jefferson rejected monarchy and the belief that some men were born to rule over others. However, he and Locke both believed that man has natural rights.

5. Analysis: (1), In the quotation, Michelangelo is saying that an uncarved block of marble is the blank slate for an artist's ideas. Therefore, Michelangelo's point of view is that each new sculpture offered an opportunity for greatness.

LESSON 4, *pp. 56–57*

1. Analysis: (1), The information states that Britain had expanded its colonial interests in India and that was the reason for the Great Trigonometrical Survey. Add that information to the fact that Nepal and Tibet refused to allow British surveyors on their land and you can draw the conclusion that they were worried about British colonial ambitions.

2. Analysis: (3), Because explorers experienced great difficulty in crossing the continent, you can conclude that the British were anxious to explore Australia's rivers because they were searching for an easy way to explore the continent's interior.

3. Analysis: (2), Britain had a history of colonization and you know that they established colonies in Australia. Therefore, you can conclude that European explorers likely experienced conflict with Aboriginal (native) Australians because the Aborigines feared British imperial ambitions. The word *imperial* is related to the word *empire*.

4. Analysis: (5), Because each expedition experienced problems, and because the South Pole is extremely cold, you can conclude that the greatest obstacle to reaching the South Pole was most likely cold temperatures.

UNIT 3 (continued)

LESSON 5, pp. 58–59

1. Analysis: (4), Because the question asked what directly led to the Nazi Party receiving the most votes in the 1932 German elections, you should determine which event occurred right before the election on the timeline. In this case, it was because the Germans were unhappy with other politicians because of the economic crisis.

2. Analysis: (3), It is clear by the events on the timeline that Germany met with little resistance to its invasions of European countries. Therefore, the trend supported by the information on the timeline is that Germany showed its strength, and many European countries gave in.

3. Evaluation: (5), Think of reasons why the European countries were reluctant to stop Hitler and the Germans. Remember that most western European nations suffered tremendous casualties and economic turmoil because of World War I. These memories were still fresh for most of their leaders. They were obviously reluctant to stop the Germans for fear of another war. Therefore, the prior event which most affected the actions shown on the timeline was World War I. You may conclude that Hitler's election as chancellor affected Germany's aggressive behavior, but that alone does not explain the appeasement strategies of the other European countries. It can also be argued that Hitler's rise was possible because of Germany's humiliation after World War I.

4. Analysis: (4), The only correct conclusion in the answer choices is number 4. You can determine this because Germany began attacking the British during the Battle of Britain. The last event on the timeline also states that Hitler called off a ground invasion of Britain. None of this would have been necessary if Britain had surrendered.

5. Evaluation: (1), Based on the information in the timeline, you can conclude that because he easily forced the surrender of Belgian forces and reached an armistice with France, Hitler was confident of victory during the summer of 1940 when he began the Battle of Britain.

LESSON 6, pp. 60–61

1. Comprehension: (1), The text states that people attempting to cross from East Germany into West Berlin mostly lost their lives. This is a generalization. The author is saying that East Germans generally did not cross successfully from East Germany to West Berlin.

2. Comprehension: (1), Answer choice 1 is the correct generalization because it is supported by details in each bullet point. Choices 2 and 5 are not correct (don't be fooled by the word 'generally'), choice 3 is a fact, not a generalization, and choice 4 cannot be proven true.

3. Application: (2), All of these nations involved in the agreement were located in Eastern Europe. They were all part of communist Yugoslavia. While all of the countries agreed to prosecute war crimes, there is no reason to assume that all of the countries were guilty of war crimes. That would be an invalid generalization.

4. Analysis: (4), The United Kingdom (UK) is part of the European Union, but is not listed as a country that uses the euro. The UK still uses the British pound as their currency.

5. Application: (1), Because the information deals primarily with economics, you can assume it is correct that countries generally joined the European Union for economic reasons.

UNIT 3 REVIEW, pp. 62–67

1. Analysis: (3), The timeline shows that China, Britain, and the Soviet Union were writing proposals for the U.N. Charter from August to October 1944. During that same time, World War II was taking place.

2. Application: (5), Because of what was happening in the world during the establishment of the United Nations, it is logical to assume that the nations were eager to form the organization because they wanted to help rebuild Europe after World War II and forestall another war.

3. Analysis: (5), Because James Cook studied the fertile land of Australia in 1770, it is logical to conclude that the British were interested in Australia because they hoped to farm the fertile soil. In fact, the information states that wheat became an important agricultural product in the early part of the 1800s.

4. Analysis: (2), You can conclude that, if the British went to the trouble of sending some of its criminals all the way to Australia, the British penal system was under strain.

5. Comprehension: (3), You can conclude that, because communities began supporting the arts, and artists began to merge their art with concepts of math and science, the arts generally became more supported and respected during the Renaissance.

6. Analysis: (1), It is clear by the description of new techniques and the combining of art with mathematics and science that the author views the Renaissance as a period of innovation.

7. Evaluation: (3), Because the information states that the British expanded their power in India and that the British military officers commanded an army in India, you can conclude that India gained its independence from Britain.

8. Application: (4), The main ideas of this information are related to British trade and control in India. These ideas are best categorized as colonialism.

9. Evaluation: (2), The diagram states that the Inca extended their influence over other groups between 1200 and 1440, or a period of more than 200 years.

10. Evaluation: (2), This information comes after the fact that the Inca gradually expanded their influence and before the period of civil war. Therefore, it should be placed between the first and second boxes.

11. Evaluation: (4), Because the Greeks told a wide variety of stories about Greek gods, Greek mythology could best be described as varied.

12. Analysis: (5), The second paragraph clearly states that Roman mythology was influenced by Greek mythology.

13. Evaluation: (4), You can conclude that the majority of Eastern European countries did not join the European Union until 2004 because before then they had been part of the Soviet Union.

UNIT 3 (continued)

14. Comprehension: (1), By reading the table carefully, you can determine that the only correct answer choice is that Ireland joined the organization more than 20 years before Hungary. Ireland joined in 1973, and Hungary joined in 2004—a difference of 31 years.

15. Evaluation: (1), Hobbes discusses the peaceful nature of man, but also concludes that people should use whatever means necessary to defend themselves.

16. Application: (2), Because Hobbes believes that man should "seek and use all helps and advantages of war" if peace cannot be maintained, his writings would be best used to support the point of view of a monarch offering protection in exchange for reduced individual rights.

17. Comprehension: (4), The information states that the Shang Dynasty was considered the first historical dynasty because the earliest written records from ancient China date from this period. In general, "historical record" is written record.

18. Application: (2), Because most of the writings and carvings relate to predictions made by Shang Dynasty kings, they are best categorized as political.

19. Analysis: (5), While all of the answer choices can be considered causes of World War I, the extensive alliances formed among nations was the cause that turned the conflict that started World War I into a world war. Those alliances brought countries not directly related to the initial conflict between Austria-Hungary and Serbia into the war.

20. Application: (4), Remember that during wartime, industries are needed to produce military items such as weapons and ammunition. You can also assume that most men who worked in those factories were needed to fight the war. Therefore, while women took over jobs left by men in many areas, the most logical answer is that women most likely worked as industrial workers.

21. Analysis: (3), The diagram indicates that Britain was anxious to keep its colonial territories and feared that Germany may win the war and dominate Western Europe. The arms race between Germany and Britain was very competitive. Therefore, you can conclude that rivalry between Britain and Germany became an important cause of World War I.

22. Application: (4), While this is not listed on the diagram, it is possible to draw the conclusion that when other European nations refused to fight Hitler (the process of appeasing him so that he was able to take over countries such as Poland without threat of war), tensions and conflicts eventually led to World War II.

UNIT 4 U.S. GOVERNMENT/CIVICS

LESSON 1, pp. 70–71

1. Comprehension: (3), The sentence discusses regulatory matters, which signals *regulations*. The most logical choice is that jurisdiction probably means the right to regulate, or make judgments.

2. Comprehension: (4), The key terms in this question are *members at large*, meaning "from any part of the city," and *successor*, which means "a newly elected member." The sentence that restates the details in the charter is choice 4.

3. Comprehension: (2), Because the states are only empowered to call on their militias at a time of war, it is logical to assume that keeping a peacetime army is a federal power.

4. Comprehension: (3), Alimony and child support are types of *other income*. Mortgages and personal loans are types of debt. The sentence states that an applicant does not have to report other income if he or she does not want it considered as a basis for repaying *this obligation*. The *obligation* refers to the credit card debt incurred if the applicant is approved. Remember, this is a credit card application.

5. Evaluation: (4), Because this is a credit application, and several of the questions deal with income, the creditor is probably most concerned with your ability to pay debt.

LESSON 2, pp. 72–73

1. Comprehension: (4), The term *domestic* in this excerpt means "within the nation." Therefore, "insure domestic tranquility" means to maintain peace within the nation.

2. Evaluation: (2), The terms "we the people" and "do ordain and establish" signify that the Preamble is a declaration.

3. Analysis: (5), The last sentence in Article I explains that Congress can override the president's veto through approval from two-thirds of both Houses.

4. Application: (2), Article I states that "all bills for raising revenue shall originate in the House." Therefore, the Senate could not introduce a bill that institutes a higher tax on gasoline.

5. Analysis: (4), Amendment IX basically states that even though the Constitution describes certain rights, it does not mean that citizens do not have additional rights.

6. Application: (2), The Ninth Amendment is often seen as a catch-all. It has been used to support the right to privacy. All other answer choices are specifically addressed in other Amendments.

LESSON 3, pp. 74–75

1. Evaluation: (1), The text clearly shows that Kennedy supported service programs.

2. Evaluation: (4), This excerpt presents facts; it is not a personal narrative. It is most like the information found in a biography.

3. Evaluation: (3), This information comes from a well-known encyclopedia and is very balanced.

4. Evaluation: (3), The U.S. Bureau of the Census is a federal government agency.

5. Evaluation: (2), Choice 2 is both biased and prejudiced. It is not supported by any information in the graph.

LESSON 4, pp. 76–77

1. Analysis: (2), Paulson states in his opening sentence that "the underlying weakness in our financial system today is the illiquid mortgage assets."

UNIT 4 (continued)

2. Analysis: (5), The language of the Act states that it was designed to combat the problem of loss of wilderness due to increasing growth and development.

3. Analysis: (2), The solution provided in the Act is to establish protected wilderness areas.

4. Analysis: (4), This amendment addresses the lack of presidential term limits.

5. Application: (3), Only Franklin Delano Roosevelt served more than two terms as president. Also, the amendment was ratified in 1951, before Kennedy, Nixon, Ford, and Lyndon B. Johnson served as president.

LESSON 5, pp. 78–79

1. Comprehension: (4), Texas is located in the 11th District. Dallas provides a clue for the location.

2. Analysis: (2), Illinois had more than 12 million people in 2000, the highest of all of the states on the map.

3. Evaluation: (3), Ohio and Michigan had a combined population of more than 20 million in 2000.

4. Analysis: (3), Congressional districts are divided by population so that representation across a given state is equal. Therefore, each district in Arkansas would have approximately the same population.

5. Analysis: (5), Each state is given (apportioned) a certain number of Representatives (1 per district) based on the population of each state and the total number of Representatives (435).

LESSON 6, pp. 80–81

1. Analysis: (3), The statement about the U.S. extending its freedom to the world is an opinion. Unlike the other answer choices, it cannot be proven true or untrue.

2. Analysis: (1), Defenders of the Electoral College can use the fact that in the long history of presidential elections, the Electoral College has only failed to select the winner of the popular vote three times.

3. Analysis: (4), One of the main opinions of the critics of the Electoral College is that it is no longer needed.

4. Analysis: (2), Campaign posters feature opinions in order to appeal to the emotions of the voters. This poster does not provide details about the candidates' platform.

5. Analysis: (1), The poster states "for lasting peace," but it is a fact that Roosevelt had taken the country into World War II.

LESSON 7, pp. 82–83

1. Evaluation: (3), A military defeat of a liberation movement in Asia would prove Castro's statement that nothing could stop a liberation movement in the contemporary world to be faulty reasoning.

2. Evaluation: (1), Because this order was issued in 1942 (when the United States was at war with Japan), Japanese Americans were affected by this order.

3. Evaluation: (4), The hasty generalization was that all people whose ancestry traces to an enemy nation are worthy of suspicion. There was no reason for the government to assume that all Japanese Americans would spy for Japan.

4. Evaluation: (4), The oversimplification here is that all criticism of the government should be treated as a crime. Pasternak was being punished (like a criminal in the cartoon) for doing so.

LESSON 8, pp. 84–85

1. Evaluation: (2), The newspaper itself states that "we exaggerate very little when we say that [Reagan] has saved the state from bankruptcy," but the commercial claims that the newspaper said "Reagan has saved the state from bankruptcy." Therefore, the claims made in the commercial are slightly exaggerated.

2. Evaluation: (2), The positive details about America show that the purpose of the information in the excerpt was to foster a sense of well-being and encourage the reelection of Bill Clinton, the Democratic president in 1996.

3. Evaluation: (4), The claim that the deficit is lower is the easiest to support with facts.

4. Evaluation: (2), The author of the editorial cites the No Child Left Behind Act to support George W. Bush's domestic policy accomplishments.

5. Evaluation: (5), Newspapers endorse candidates in editorials to explain why the editorial staff supports one candidate over the others. This editorial was designed to convince people to vote for George W. Bush.

LESSON 9, pp. 86–87

1. Analysis: (3), McCain could have strengthened his argument by providing details from both his and his opponent's proposed federal budgets.

2. Analysis: (3), Fulbright uses his beliefs about the President's intent to support his argument when he says "I think it would indicate that he [Johnson] would take reasonable means first to prevent any further aggression. . . "

3. Analysis: (1), Gruening argues that the resolution will lead to unchecked U.S. aggression in Southeast Asia when he says that the President may see fit to move troops into countries other than Vietnam.

4. Analysis: (4), Obama strengthens his argument by providing details about the economic improvements made during the last Democratic administration when he discusses progress during Bill Clinton's presidency.

UNIT 4 REVIEW, pp. 88–93

1. Analysis: (2), While many believe that this was true, it obviously cannot be proven true that if Perot had not entered the election, Bush would have been reelected as president.

2. Analysis: (5), Only answer choice 5 is a primary source.

3. Analysis: (4), The second paragraph explains that affirmative action programs were established to address the harmful effects of past discrimination.

4. Evaluation: (3), The root word of *inviolable* is *violate*. Therefore, *inviolable* means "safe from violation."

5. Analysis: (2), The details in Section 3 show that the main focus of this section is the formation of new states.

6. Evaluation: (1), Read the sentence to determine the context. The best substitution for be *convened* is *meet*.

UNIT 4 (continued)

7. Analysis: (1), Bush opens and closes his remarks by discussing his presidential experience.

8. Evaluation: (5), Bush claims that children no longer go to bed at night fearing a nuclear war. Bush uses this example to claim that he solved a foreign policy problem.

9. Evaluation: (3), The second paragraph of Clinton's statement includes details about economic improvements in Arkansas during his tenure as governor. Clinton uses these statistics to strengthen his argument.

10. Analysis: (4), The only statement that can be proven is that there have been twice as many bankruptcies as new jobs created.

11. Analysis: (3), Because the cartoonist is showing a voter putting money in a ballot box, he is drawing attention to the increasing importance of campaign fundraising in the electoral process.

12. Evaluation: (4), This source, like most political cartoons, can be best described as commentary.

13. Evaluation: (1), The New York Times is a very reputable publication. That is why this editorial should be respected.

14. Evaluation: (2), In the second paragraph, the author claims that John McCain "is shuffling in step with his restrictionist party" regarding immigration.

15. Evaluation: (5), The figures in the cartoon seem to be in charge of giving a literacy test, yet cannot themselves read the word *literacy*. These figures demonstrate faulty logic because an honest literacy test would prevent them from voting.

16. Analysis: (4), Literacy tests were just one way that Southern states tried to prevent African Americans from voting before the success of the civil rights movement. Often white voters were given very simple tests, while African Americans who attempted to vote would be given extremely difficult ones. By pointing out the unfairness of this, the cartoonist is making a statement about civil rights.

17. Analysis: (2), The only hard statistics quoted in the platform were related to the economy. Therefore, the claim best supported by the facts is that twenty years ago, the economy was in shambles.

18. Evaluation: (3), The party platform is biased because it discusses the New Economy, but does not include the accomplishments of President Clinton's eight years in office.

19. Comprehension: (1), According to the map key, the shading for Indiana means that on the date the poll was taken, McCain was leading in Indiana.

20. Analysis: (4), The map shows that Obama had at least some support in the Northeast, the Great Lakes, the Midwest, the South, and the West—in all regions of the country.

21. Comprehension: (2), If the election were held the day this poll was taken, Obama would have won. He was leading in more states, but more importantly, he would have received far more electoral votes.

22. Analysis: (2), During the election, political pundits and others discussed how the changing demographics (more people moving south and west from states in the Northeast and Midwest—states more traditionally Democratic) were one of the reasons for Obama's support in traditionally Republican states such as North Carolina and Colorado.

UNIT 5 ECONOMICS

LESSON 1, *pp. 96–97*

1. Analysis: (5), In the cartoon, the lemonade stand represents a small business, so therefore it represents microeconomics. The kids running the lemonade stand comment about their place in the entire U.S. economy—macroeconomics. Therefore, the cartoon illustrates a connection between microeconomics and macroeconomics.

2. Comprehension: (3), The information states that Smith believed that a country's economy works best when its government does not interfere with it. Therefore, he believed that the best economies are free market economies.

3. Analysis: (1), Because Smith believed that the government should not interfere with business, it is logical to conclude that he thought that government should remove obstacles to business growth.

4. Comprehension: (2), The first sentence in the excerpt tells you that Smith believes that a nation's wealth is produced by the labor of its workforce.

5. Comprehension: (2), Except in times of economic turmoil, the type of economic system most often practiced in the United States is *laissez-faire* capitalism.

6. Analysis: (1), Because Keynes believed that the government should make investments in society and businesses to spur the economy, you can conclude that during the Great Depression Keynes believed that the United States government should create jobs to lower unemployment.

LESSON 2, *pp. 98–99*

1. Application: (4), The transformation process implies that something transforms, or changes, into something else. In a candle-making business, melting the wax, inserting the wicks, molding the wax, and letting it cool would transform wax and string into candles.

2. Evaluation: (4), According to the business cycle, investment (home buying) would be the highest during the recovery and prosperity phases.

3. Analysis: (2), An economic stimulation of some type is required to move from the depression phase to the recovery phase.

4. Analysis: (4), The prosperity phase is most associated with continued economic growth.

5. Application: (3), New Deal legislation created jobs and a social safety net for retirees and those without health care. The outbreak of World War II stimulated the economy with a huge increase in manufactured goods necessary to fight the war.

LESSON 3, *pp. 100–101*

1. Comprehension: (2), Except for in the 1980s, the developing world has always had a higher real and projected inflation rate. Therefore, the developing world is most affected by inflation.

2. Analysis: (5), According to the information, supply, demand, and inflation are each influenced by many causes.

3. Analysis: (1), Supply and demand require competition to function freely. Competition helps regulate prices and the supply of goods. Also, if demand is higher, more companies will start producing an item, which can help drive prices down to the equilibrium point.

4. Analysis: (3), If both price and supply are above the equilibrium point, then both price and supply will go down. If there is too much of an item on the market, producers will stop making as much of the item (reducing supply) and cut the price so that more consumers will buy the item (reducing price).

5. Analysis: (4), Price regulation interferes with the free market philosophy. Price is no longer based on supply, demand, and competition. Therefore, if potential profit is limited by a price regulation, fewer companies will have the incentive to produce the goods.

LESSON 4, *pp. 102–103*

1. Analysis: (5), For this question, compare the median home prices in the table with the changes in household income on the map. The states that suffered the largest decrease in household income were Colorado, Washington, and Oregon. Compared with the median home prices in those three states, you can conclude that because Colorado has the highest prices of the three, its residents might have the most difficulty affording a new home.

2. Analysis: (4), By comparing the data in the table and the graph, the only logical choice is that there is a connection between level of education and degree of economic success.

3. Analysis: (1), Because around 25% of Indiana residents aged 25 to 34 have a Bachelor's degree or higher, it is possible that that group earns on average more than $56,000 per year.

4. Evaluation: (3), Because the bar graph does not distinguish between percentages of Indiana residents with a Bachelor's Degree or an advanced degree, you cannot determine the percentage of Indiana residents with an earning potential of more than $82,000 per year.

5. Analysis: (2), Based on the data in the table, Braden's average annual earnings potential is around $30,000.

LESSON 5, *pp. 104–105*

1. Analysis: (2), Even though the data in the two circle graphs is not the exact same, the figures are very similar. Therefore, you can conclude that the United States and Canada have similar economies. No GDP figures are provided, only percentages of an unknown total GDP.

2. Analysis: (4), This line graph illustrates that there is no single trend (gradual increase or gradual decrease) in the U.S. unemployment rate from 1948–2007. Instead, the trend shows that the nation has experienced alternating periods of rising and falling unemployment over time.

3. Analysis: (3), Because the unemployment rate is often linked to recession, and the years of highest unemployment on the graph were between 1978 and 1984, you can assume that the period in which the United States likely experienced its most severe recession of the past 60 years was from 1978 to 1984.

4. Analysis: (1), Because the Dow increased dramatically between 1995 and 2000, it is most likely that the U.S. economy grew significantly stronger during that period.

5. Analysis: (4), Despite the fact that the Dow decreased by a larger percentage in 2000 than in 1990, the average at the start of 2000 was significantly larger than that of 1990, indicating that the economy was stronger overall that year.

LESSON 6, *pp. 106–107*

1. Comprehension: (3), By examining the pictograph and the key, you can determine that the value of goods traded between the United States and Japan was approximately $200 billion.

2. Comprehension: (2), If each gas pump symbol represents 10 percent of the total retail price of gasoline, then federal and state taxes represent approximately 15 percent of the total cost.

3. Analysis: (5), Because the price of crude oil represents more than 50 percent of the total price of a gallon of gas, a decrease in the price of crude oil would have the greatest effect on the cost of a gallon of gas.

4. Comprehension: (1), The corn symbols each represent $1 billion, and Iowa has nine solid corn symbols and part of another one. Therefore, you can determine that the value of corn production in Iowa in 2007 exceeded $9 billion.

5. Analysis: (4), Look closely at the states listed on the pictograph. These are the top corn producing states in the United States. All of the states are in the Midwest. Therefore, you can conclude that the Midwest grows most of the corn produced in the United States.

LESSON 7, *pp. 108–109*

1. Evaluation: (4), The red bars represent the average mortgage rate. Between 1990 and 2000, the average mortgage rate dropped by about 2 percent.

2. Evaluation: (3), Because M2 is M1 plus savings deposits worth less than $100,000, M2 will always be greater than M1.

3. Comprehension: (1), The black line represents M1. According to the graph, the value of M1 in 1970 was approximately $200 billion.

4. Comprehension: (5), The red line represents M2. The value of M2 over M1 was the greatest in 2000.

5. Analysis: (5), Because liquidity is measured in how easily items can be turned into cash, the economy probably had the most liquidity when the value of M1 (which is made up of cash, traveler's checks, and checking accounts) was highest—2000.

UNIT 5 (continued)

LESSON 8, pp. 110–111

1. Analysis: (3), For this question, you must decide which country produced the greatest number of people with engineering degrees, yet had the lowest annual salaries. According to the graphs, you can predict that a U.S. corporation could find the best combination of highly trained yet affordable prospective employees in China.

2. Analysis: (3), Because telecommuters would be working separately from other employees, they would have the most difficulty participating in team building exercises.

3. Analysis: (4), Because the number of telecommuters increased dramatically between 1990 and 1997, you can predict that the number of telecommuters continued to increase steadily in the years after 1997.

4. Analysis: (4), If the U.S. automakers had been allowed to fail, then more cars would have to be imported, which would have a negative impact on international trade.

UNIT 5 REVIEW, pp. 112–117

1. Analysis: (3), The economic crisis in 1991 caused India to institute significant economic reforms.

2. Application: (1), India's railway industry is controlled by the government. In the United States, the government controls primary and secondary education through local school districts.

3. Analysis: (3), Socialism is an economic system in which the government controls some aspects of the economy deemed vital to the nation. In India, socialism is represented by the government's control of nuclear power.

4. Analysis: (2), While some of the answer choices may reduce the national debt, only choice 2 would guarantee a reduction because it would produce a surplus specifically for reducing debt. There is no reason to assume that money saved by cutting government programs would be used to pay off the national debt.

5. Analysis: (4), This pictograph can be tricky. The gray circles represent $100 billion whereas the red blocks represent $1 trillion. By analyzing the pictograph carefully, you can determine that the national debt level has continued to rise since 1970.

6. Comprehension: (4), The pictograph shows the national debt level in 1995 as 4 complete red boxes and 2/3 of another. This represents approximately $4.7 trillion dollars.

7. Application: (3), Because the information states that telecommuting will save costs in a number of areas, you can predict that government work will be completed more affordably through further implementation of telework.

8. Analysis: (3), The information states that if the people's purchasing power is weakened, an economic depression can get worse. When a depression increases, the Gross Domestic Product (GDP) can decrease. When examining the Real GDP in the table, you can see that it decreases in the early years of the 1930s. Therefore, you can conclude that the purchasing power of U.S. consumers grew increasingly weak during the early 1930s.

9. Analysis: (5), Remember that World War II began in Europe in 1939 and the U.S. supplied their European allies with goods, therefore increasing demand. This would only increase when the United States entered the war. An increased demand for industrial goods would lead to a decrease in unemployment.

10. Evaluation: (1), To make an accurate comparison, historians and economists often list economic figures in current value. They are adjusting for inflation.

11. Analysis: (4), Labor is another word for work, so the work of the lawnmower company's employees would be considered labor.

12. Application: (5), An entrepreneur is someone who displays the willingness to start one's own business.

13. Comprehension: (2), According to the flowchart, firms generate revenue (earn money) by selling goods and services to people in households.

14. Analysis: (2), All four corners of the flowchart show examples of how all transactions between firms and households contribute to the nation's GDP.

15. Analysis: (3), An increase in the number of wildfires and a decrease in citrus production can both be linked to a nationwide drought.

16. Application: (1), A nationwide drought could also have produced higher vegetable prices. You can assume that in a drought, farmers would produce fewer vegetables. Remember that lower supply can lead to higher prices.

17. Comprehension: (2), The graph shows that the year in which citrus production was the highest was 2004.

18. Comprehension: (4), The line graph shows that the greatest increase in U.S. wildfires occurred between 2005 and 2006.

19. Analysis: (3), By examining the graphs, you can determine that both provide information about the economic status of individual states.

20. Evaluation: (3), Because both graphs show a gradual increase, you can determine that the period from 2007 to 2011 would likely feature steady increases in GDP and per capita income for each state.

21. Evaluation: (4), *Per capita* means "per person," so the second graph takes the entire income of the state and divides that by the population of that state. The first graph shows that Ohio has a much higher GDP than Connecticut, but in the second graph, Connecticut has a much higher per capita income. Therefore, you can conclude that Connecticut has a smaller population than Ohio.

22. Evaluation: (5), The multi-line graph takes the population of each state into account when measuring data. That is why it is called "per capita income by state." The multi-bar graph does not take the state's population into account.

Index

Note: Page numbers in **boldface** indicate definitions or main discussion. Page numbers in *italic* indicate a visual representation. Page ranges indicate examples and practice.

G

H

I

INDEX

Information
- analyzing sources of, **74**, 74–75
- categorizing, *26*
- displayed in charts/graphs, *34–35*
- distinguishing fact and opinion, 80
- drawing conclusions from, 56
- drawing conclusions from multiple sources, **104**, 104–105
- evaluation of, **84**, 84–85
- inferences based on, 36
- organization in tables, 22
- sequencing, 28–29, 52

Interest rates, *108*, 109

Interpreting
- charts and graphs, **34**, 34–35
- diagrams, **52**, 52–53
- flowcharts, **98**, 98–990
- multi-bar/multi-line graphs, **108**, 108–109
- pictographs, **106**, 106–107
- political cartoons, **38**, 38–39
- special-purpose maps, **78**, 78–79
- tables, **22**, 22–23
- timelines, **58**, 58–59

Intervals on timelines, 58

Iowa, *107*

Ireland
- EU membership, 61, *65*
- salary of software programmers in, *110*

Israel, *110*

Italy
- declaration of war on France/Britain, *59*
- EU membership, 61, *65*

J

Jackson, Andrew, 28–29
Japan, *106*, *110*
Jay, John, 27, 44
Jefferson, Thomas, 25, *26*, 44
Johnson, Lyndon B., *43*, 87
Judgments, 56, 84, 104
Justice system
- of England, 52
- U.S. Supreme Court, 28, 75

K

Kennedy, John F., 40, *43*, 74
Kerry, John, 85
Key
- on double bar graphs, 108
- on maps, 4, 6, 8
- for pictographs, 106
Keynes, John Maynard, 97
Keynesian economists, 97
Keywords
- indicating absolutes/universals, 12
- indicating cause/effect relationships, 30
- indicating generalizations, 60
- indicating order of events/process, 28
- signaling comparisons/contrasts, 32

Korean War, *41*

L

Labels
- information in, 74
- on maps, 4
- on political cartoons, *38–39*
Labor, 114
Laissez-faire, 97
Lake Erie, Battle of, *29*
Landforms, 6
Laos, 87
Latitude, lines of, 4
Latvia, *65*
League of Nations, *39*, 67
Lee, Robert E., 33
Leviathan (Hobbes), 66
Lincoln, Abraham
- Lincoln-Douglas debate, 45
- Reconstruction plan, 32, *33*
Lincoln-Douglas debate, 45
Line graphs
- of U.S. employment rates, *105*
- interpreting charts and graphs, **34**, 34
- of manufacturing growth in Illinois, *34*
- of population of Michigan, *44*
- of U.S. wildfires, *116*
- *See also* Multi-line graphs
Lines
- of latitude, **4**
- of longitude, **4**
- on maps (indicating movement), 10
Liquidation phase, *99*
Lithuania, *65*
Locke, John, 55
Logic, faulty, **82**, 82–84
Longitude, lines of, 4
Luxembourg, 61, *65*

M

Macroeconomics, *96*
Madison, James, 44
Magna Carta, *52*, 54
Maine, 46
Main idea
- details and, **24**, 24–25
- summarizing and, 40
Making assumptions, x–xiii
- about chronological order, 28
- about commentary of political cartoons, 38
- about inflation, 100
- about logical statements, 82
- about role of labor in production, 98
- boundaries on physical maps, 6
- comparing/contrasting parallel items, 32
- exclude answers with *all, none, every, never*, 12
- interpreting pictographs, 106
Making inferences, **36**, 36–37

Malaysia, *110*
Malta, 61, *65*
Manufacturing, 30, *34*
Maps
- of 2008 electoral college polls, *93*
- of African refugee areas in 2004, *12*
- Alabama precipitation, *7*
- Arizona, *9*
- of Arkansas's congressional districts, *79*
- of Athens and Sparta, *51*
- Atlantic slave trade routes, *10*
- Australia, *5*
- of Battle of Friedland, *19*
- California physical, *6*
- Canada population, *16*
- definition of, **2**
- Eastern Hemisphere, *xvi–xvii*, *14*
- equator, *xii*, *2*
- Europe in 1914 and 1919, *13*
- of Federal Reserve districts, *78*
- Georgia highways, *3*, *5*
- of Gettysburg battle on third day, *13*
- of Great Migration in U. S., *17*
- key, 4, 6
- of Korean War, *41*
- lines of latitude/longitude, **4**
- map components, **4**, 4–5
- of median household income, *102*
- Michigan natural features, *7*
- movement on, **10**, 10–11, *13*, *17*, *19*, *41*, *43*
- New Jersey, *4*
- physical maps, **6**, 6–7, *7*, **8**, *15*, *18*
- political maps, *xiv–xvii*, *2*, *3*, 4–5, 8–9, *13*, *14*, *16*, 51
- population of Midwest states, *79*
- of precipitation in U.S., *18*
- of regions of Ecuador, *2*
- scales, *4*
- of settlement of Ohio, *19*
- of Silk Road, *11*
- of slave trade routes, *10*
- Spain population, *9*
- special-purpose maps, 78–79, *93*, *102*
- special-purpose maps, interpreting, **78**, 78–79
- symbols on, **4**, 6
- of United States, *xiv*, *18*
- United States Southern region, *15*
- Western Hemisphere, *xv*
- of westward trails in U.S., *43*
- Wyoming, *8*
Maryland
- as a colony, *22*, *23*
- signers of Declaration of Independence, *25*
Massachusetts
- as a colony, *22*, *23*
- signers of Declaration of Independence, *25*
McCain, John, 86, 91, *93*
McCarthy, Joseph, 41
Mexico, 29, *106*
Michelangelo Buonaroti, ***Sonnet 15***, 55
Michigan, *7*, 44
Michigan, Lake, *7*

INDEX

U

V

W

X

Y